GUNFIGHTER®

FUNDAMENTAL CARBINE

Warm Ups, Drills, Exercises and Quals

NAME: _____

UNIT: _____

Weapon Conditions

- Condition 4: No mag inserted. Slide forward on empty chamber. Hammer forward (if applicable). Weapon on safe (if applicable).

- Condition 3: Loaded mag inserted. Slide forward on empty chamber. Hammer forward (if applicable). Weapon on safe (if applicable).

- Condition 2: Loaded mag inserted. Slide forward with round in chamber. Hammer forward (if applicable). Weapon on safe (if applicable).

- Condition 1: Loaded mag inserted. Slide forward with round in chamber. Hammer cocked (if applicable). Weapon on safe (if applicable).

Always know the condition of your weapon!

Safety

- Treat every weapon as if it were loaded.
- Never point your weapon at anything you do not intend to shoot/destroy.
- Know your target and it's background.
- Keep your finger off the trigger until you intend to fire.
- Keep your weapon on safe until you are ready to fire.
- Always wear eye and ear protection, and proper protective clothing.
- Never shoot faster than you can effectively keep rounds on target.
- Be extremely cautious with back splatter and ricochets when shooting steel.

Warning

Perform these drills at your own risk. Only perform these drill in a safe manner which do not violate your range rules. Consult range staff for rules and regulations regarding drawing from a holster, rapid fire and multiple target engagements.

GUNFIGHTER is not responsible for any injury or death that may occur due to the use of this book. We recommend never shooting alone and under supervision of trained safety officers.

Table of Contents:

Admin and Logistics.

Warm Up Drills.
Ready Drills

Manipulation Drills.
Load & Unload that Carbine

Stack It

Feed It

Carbine Push Pull…

Carbine Dublin

10 x 5

Go To Gun

Accuracy Drills.
Trigger Effect

Solid Shot

5 For 10

Pin Point

Rock Solid

Ready Positions Drills.
Carbine Low Ready

Carbine Ready

Carbine High Ready

Carbine Port Ready

Carbine Tactical Ready

Recoil Management Drills.
Under Control

Sledge Hammer

Gas It

Cadence Count

Positional Drills.
Prone Out

Take A Knee

Stand Your Ground

Rice Paddy

Multiple Target Drills.
Rhodie Mike

Rake'm

Reality Hits The Fan

Speedy

Gun Fighting Skill Drills.
Gang Land

In The Line Of Fire

Service Time

Course Of Fire Quals.
Gunfighter Standard 1

Gunfighter Standard 2

Custom Drill

Notes

Class Contacts and Notes

www.GUNFIGHTERSERIES.com ©

How to use this book:

This book offers a carefully crafted catalog of training drills and is designed to log and track training progression as well as shot pattern placement analysis. **All targets may be downloaded for free** of our www.GunfighterSereis.com website and printed at home for free with the exception of the JD-QUAL1 target which may be purchased at numerous online retailers. The JD-Qual1 target may also be substituted with a cardboard IPSC with a rectangular body A zone.

For best results, conduct and record every drill at least once starting at the beginning. The more data you collect the better your results will be.

Most drills offer defensive time and scoring goals to achieve. Competitive shooters may set different goals. Everyone's goal should be to improve their recorded personal best.

For proper weapons handling and marksmanship coaching, seek out well respected firearms instructors and courses.

Train safe. Train hard. Train to win.

Afterwards:

Upon mastering all the drills in this book, continue to increase your skills by utilizing the entire Gunfighter training log book series.

Gunfighter Skill Books 2016 © - Gunfighter, LLC - All Rights Reserved

ISBN: 9781076724205   Revised 2019

Round Count Log

Weapon Make & Model: SN#:

Date	Ammo	Lot #	Fired	Total

Date	Ammo	Lot #	Fired	Total

This Page	
Previous Page	
TOTAL	

Notes:

Round Count Log

www.GUNFIGHTERSERIES.com ©

Weapon Make & Model: SN#:

Date	Ammo	Lot #	Fired	Total	Date	Ammo	Lot #	Fired	Total

This Page	
Previous Page	
TOTAL	

Notes:

Round Count Log

Weapon Make & Model: SN#:

Date	Ammo	Lot #	Fired	Total

Date	Ammo	Lot #	Fired	Total

This Page	
Previous Page	
TOTAL	

Notes:

Admin & Logistics - 4

Fundamental Carbine ©

Round Count Log

www.GUNFIGHTERSERIES.com ©

Weapon Make & Model:

SN#:

Date	Ammo	Lot #	Fired	Total

Date	Ammo	Lot #	Fired	Total

This Page	
Previous Page	
TOTAL	

Notes:

Maintenance Log

Weapon Make & Model: _____ SN#: _____

Date	Full Cleaning	Damage Inspection
	Y / N	Y / N
	Y / N	Y / N
	Y / N	Y / N
	Y / N	Y / N
	Y / N	Y / N
	Y / N	Y / N
	Y / N	Y / N
	Y / N	Y / N
	Y / N	Y / N
	Y / N	Y / N
	Y / N	Y / N
	Y / N	Y / N

Parts Replaced:

Date	Full Cleaning	Damage Inspection
	Y / N	Y / N
	Y / N	Y / N
	Y / N	Y / N
	Y / N	Y / N
	Y / N	Y / N
	Y / N	Y / N
	Y / N	Y / N
	Y / N	Y / N
	Y / N	Y / N
	Y / N	Y / N
	Y / N	Y / N
	Y / N	Y / N

Notes:

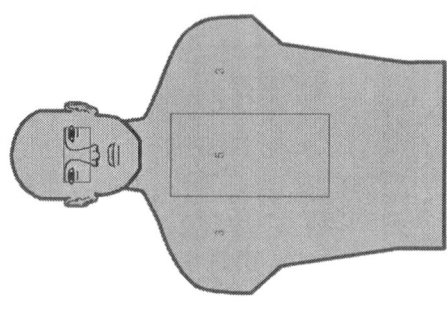

CARBINE READY WARM UP DRILLS

Purpose: Increase competency of the use of the carbine ready positions.

Distance: 25 Yards.

Target: JD-QUAL1

Total Rounds Fired: 0 Rounds.

Repetitions: 10 Reps each.

Starting Position & Condition: Standing. Condition 4.

    Low Ready Description: At your own personal go, raise the carbine and take aim at the target from the low ready position. Low ready position is where the rifle butt on your shoulder with the muzzle pointed into the dirt 6 to 8 feet in front of you while you are looking at the target.

    Ready Description: At your own personal go, raise the carbine and take aim at the target from the ready position. The ready position is where the rifle butt on your shoulder with the muzzle pointed in the direction of the target while you are looking at the target just over the top of the sights.

    High Ready Description: At your own personal go, raise the carbine, position the buttstock and take aim at the target from the high ready position. The high ready position is where the rifle butt is at the side of your hip with the muzzle pointed in the upward direction at a roughly 60 degree angle at direction of the target while you are looking at the target just over the top of the front sight.

Goals: The goal of these drills are to be smooth and deliberate.

CARBINE READY WARM UP DRILLS

Purpose: Increase competency of the use of the carbine ready positions.

Distance: 25 Yards.

Target: JD-QUAL1

Total Rounds Fired: 0 Rounds.

Repetitions: 10 Reps each.

Starting Position & Condition: Standing. Condition 4.

Port Ready Description: At your own personal go, raise the carbine, position the buttstock and take aim at the target from the port ready position. The port ready position is where the rifle butt is at your side, just above your hip, with the muzzle pointed straight upward. Your firing hand should be holding the pistol grip and you can either hold the handguard or not depending on what you want to practice.

Tactical Ready Description: At your own personal go, raise the carbine, position the buttstock and take aim at the target from the tactical ready position. The tactical ready position is where the rifle butt is in front of your shoulder, the rifle is turned on its side with the muzzle pointed in the direction of the ground 6 to 8 inches straight in front of your feet.

Ready Right / Ready Left Description: At the timer beep, perform mounting the carbine, aiming and pressing the trigger, dry firing, from any ready position you choose while moving 1 to 2 steps to the right or left within 2 seconds. This movement is to get you out of the line of fire or attack while moving laterally.

Goals: The goal of these drills are to be smooth and deliberate.

Warm Up Drill - 1

Fundamental Carbine ©

READY POSITION WARM UPS

www.GUNFIGHTERSERIES.com ©

Date:	Weapon & Sights	Low Ready X 10	Ready X 10	High Ready X 10	Port Ready X 10	Tactical Ready X 10	Ready Right X 10 Sub 2 Sec Par?	Ready Left X 10 Sub 2 Sec Par?
		Y / N	Y / N	Y / N	Y / N	Y / N	Y / N	Y / N
		Y / N	Y / N	Y / N	Y / N	Y / N	Y / N	Y / N
		Y / N	Y / N	Y / N	Y / N	Y / N	Y / N	Y / N
		Y / N	Y / N	Y / N	Y / N	Y / N	Y / N	Y / N
		Y / N	Y / N	Y / N	Y / N	Y / N	Y / N	Y / N
		Y / N	Y / N	Y / N	Y / N	Y / N	Y / N	Y / N
		Y / N	Y / N	Y / N	Y / N	Y / N	Y / N	Y / N
		Y / N	Y / N	Y / N	Y / N	Y / N	Y / N	Y / N
		Y / N	Y / N	Y / N	Y / N	Y / N	Y / N	Y / N
		Y / N	Y / N	Y / N	Y / N	Y / N	Y / N	Y / N
		Y / N	Y / N	Y / N	Y / N	Y / N	Y / N	Y / N
		Y / N	Y / N	Y / N	Y / N	Y / N	Y / N	Y / N
		Y / N	Y / N	Y / N	Y / N	Y / N	Y / N	Y / N

READY POSITION WARM UPS

Date:	Weapon & Sights	Low Ready X 10	Ready X 10	High Ready X 10	Port Ready X 10	Tactical Ready X 10	Ready Right X 10 Sub 2 Sec Par?	Ready Left X 10 Sub 2 Sec Par?
		Y / N	Y / N	Y / N	Y / N	Y / N	Y / N	Y / N
		Y / N	Y / N	Y / N	Y / N	Y / N	Y / N	Y / N
		Y / N	Y / N	Y / N	Y / N	Y / N	Y / N	Y / N
		Y / N	Y / N	Y / N	Y / N	Y / N	Y / N	Y / N
		Y / N	Y / N	Y / N	Y / N	Y / N	Y / N	Y / N
		Y / N	Y / N	Y / N	Y / N	Y / N	Y / N	Y / N
		Y / N	Y / N	Y / N	Y / N	Y / N	Y / N	Y / N
		Y / N	Y / N	Y / N	Y / N	Y / N	Y / N	Y / N
		Y / N	Y / N	Y / N	Y / N	Y / N	Y / N	Y / N
		Y / N	Y / N	Y / N	Y / N	Y / N	Y / N	Y / N
		Y / N	Y / N	Y / N	Y / N	Y / N	Y / N	Y / N
		Y / N	Y / N	Y / N	Y / N	Y / N	Y / N	Y / N
		Y / N	Y / N	Y / N	Y / N	Y / N	Y / N	Y / N

Warm Up Drill - 1

Fundamental Carbine ©

LOAD AND UNLOAD THAT CARBINE

Purpose: Increase efficiency and develop nervous system memory of loading and unloading a carbine.

Extra Equipment Needed: 5 DUMMY Rounds, 1 magazine and 1 magazine pouch.

Total Rounds Fired: 5 DUMMY Rounds.

Repetitions: 10 Reps.

Starting Position & Condition: Standing – Carbine pointing upward in front of you. Condition 4.

Description: Face in a safe direction by following the firearm safety rules. Bring the carbine magazine well up in front of your face just below your eyes so you can maintain situational awareness. Lock the butt stock into your side with your elbow tucked into your side. Take a magazine, with 5 dummy rounds in it, out of your magazine pouch and insert it into the magazine well. Push the magazine forcefully up to the point where you hear the click of the magazine being locked in place. While keeping the carbine in the same position, slide your hand up the magazine well and use your thumb to depress the bolt release and chamber a round. Perform a round press check to make sure a round is in the chamber. Push on the forward assist and close the dust cover. Unload the carbine by locking the bolt back, thus removing the round that was in the chamber and then remove the magazine. Perform a 3 point unload safety check.

Goals: The goals of this drill is to be smooth, deliberate and to remove the round in the chamber first before removing the magazine, allowing you to practice for Type 2 malfunction clearing.

LOAD & UNLOAD THAT CARBINE

Date:	Location:	Weapon:		10 Reps?	Notes:
				Y / N	
				Y / N	
				Y / N	
				Y / N	
				Y / N	
				Y / N	
				Y / N	
				Y / N	
				Y / N	
				Y / N	
				Y / N	
				Y / N	
				Y / N	
				Y / N	
				Y / N	
				Y / N	

Manipulation Drills - 1

LOAD & UNLOAD THAT CARBINE

www.GUNFIGHTERSERIES.com ©

Date:	Location:	Weapon:	10 Reps?	Notes:
			Y / N	
			Y / N	
			Y / N	
			Y / N	
			Y / N	
			Y / N	
			Y / N	
			Y / N	
			Y / N	
			Y / N	
			Y / N	
			Y / N	
			Y / N	
			Y / N	
			Y / N	
			Y / N	

LOAD & UNLOAD THAT CARBINE

Date:	Location:	Weapon:	10 Reps?	Notes:
			Y / N	
			Y / N	
			Y / N	
			Y / N	
			Y / N	
			Y / N	
			Y / N	
			Y / N	
			Y / N	
			Y / N	
			Y / N	
			Y / N	
			Y / N	
			Y / N	
			Y / N	

Manipulation Drills - 1

STACK IT

Purpose: Increase efficiency and develop nervous system memory of a tactical reload.

Extra Equipment Needed: 2 magazines, 1 magazine pouch.

Repetitions: 10 Reps.

Starting Position & Condition: Standing - Carbine pointed forward. Condition 3 with an empty magazine inserted.

Description: Face in a safe direction by following the firearm safety rules. Bring the carbine magazine well up in front of your face just below your eyes so you can maintain situational awareness. Lock the butt stock into your side with your elbow tucked into your side, take a magazine out of your magazine pouch. Create an L shape with the two magazines. Remove the magazine that is in the carbine. Insert the new magazine into the magazine well. When you insert the magazine push forcefully to the point where you hear the click of the magazine being locked in place. Tug on the magazine to verify that it is secure. Insert the magazine that was in the carbine first into the magazine pouch. Perform a scan of the area. If you have more than one magazine pouch, use the magazine farthest from the front.

Goals: Goals: The goals of this drill is to be smooth and deliberate.

STACK IT

Date:	Location:	Weapon:	10 Reps?	Notes:
			Y / N	
			Y / N	
			Y / N	
			Y / N	
			Y / N	
			Y / N	
			Y / N	
			Y / N	
			Y / N	
			Y / N	
			Y / N	
			Y / N	
			Y / N	
			Y / N	
			Y / N	
			Y / N	

Manipulation Drills - 2

STACK IT

www.GUNFIGHTERSERIES.com ©

Date:	Location:	Weapon:	10 Reps?	Notes:
			Y / N	
			Y / N	
			Y / N	
			Y / N	
			Y / N	
			Y / N	
			Y / N	
			Y / N	
			Y / N	
			Y / N	
			Y / N	
			Y / N	
			Y / N	
			Y / N	
			Y / N	

STACK IT

Date:	Location:	Weapon:	10 Reps?	Notes:
			Y / N	
			Y / N	
			Y / N	
			Y / N	
			Y / N	
			Y / N	
			Y / N	
			Y / N	
			Y / N	
			Y / N	
			Y / N	
			Y / N	
			Y / N	
			Y / N	
			Y / N	

Manipulation Drills - 2

Fundamental Carbine ©

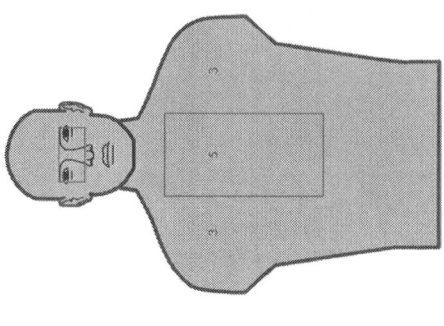

FEED IT

Purpose: Increase reloading speed, nervous system memory of an emergency reload and recoil management.

Distance: 25 Yards

Target: JD-QUAL1

Par Time: 6.5 Seconds.

Extra Equipment Needed: Shot timer, 2 magazines and 1 magazine pouch.

Rounds Fired Per Rep: 4 to 6 Rounds.   **Total Rounds Fired:** 20 to 30 Rounds.

Point Penalty: Go / No Go.

Repetitions: 5 Reps.

Starting Position & Condition: Standing – Carbine pointed at target. Condition 1 with a magazine with 1 round inserted in the carbine.

Description: At the timer beep, fire 2 rounds into the (5 point) A Zone body, reload the carbine, aim and fire 2 rounds into the (5 point) A Zone body box after reloading. Record the time. Repeat 4 more times firing the same number of rounds after reloading as the previous repetitions. Remove the high and low times and average the 3 remaining times for an average. Try different round counts on different sessions and over time, see if your average times for the same round counts are coming down. Left handed shooters add .5 seconds. From a vest add .5 seconds to par time.

Goals: Novice: 6.5 Seconds.   Expert: 5.5 Seconds.   Gunfighter: 4.5 Seconds.

FEED IT

Date:	Location:	Weapon:	Sights:	A Box: Head / Body
Rep 1 Time:	Rep 2 Time:	Rep 3 Time:	Rep 4 Time:	Rep 5 Time:
Reload Time:	Reload Time:	Reload Time:	Reload Time:	Reload Time:
A Box: Go / No Go	A Box: Go / No Go	A Box: Go / No Go	A Box: Go / No Go	A Box: Go / No Go
# of Shots:	# of Shots:	# of Shots:	# of Shots:	# of Shots:
Ave Reload Time:		Ave Total Rep Time:		Notes:

Date:	Location:	Weapon:	Sights:	A Box: Head / Body
Rep 1 Time:	Rep 2 Time:	Rep 3 Time:	Rep 4 Time:	Rep 5 Time:
Reload Time:	Reload Time:	Reload Time:	Reload Time:	Reload Time:
A Box: Go / No Go	A Box: Go / No Go	A Box: Go / No Go	A Box: Go / No Go	A Box: Go / No Go
# of Shots:	# of Shots:	# of Shots:	# of Shots:	# of Shots:
Ave Reload Time:		Ave Total Rep Time:		Notes:

Date:	Location:	Weapon:	Sights:	A Box: Head / Body
Rep 1 Time:	Rep 2 Time:	Rep 3 Time:	Rep 4 Time:	Rep 5 Time:
Reload Time:	Reload Time:	Reload Time:	Reload Time:	Reload Time:
A Box: Go / No Go	A Box: Go / No Go	A Box: Go / No Go	A Box: Go / No Go	A Box: Go / No Go
# of Shots::	# of Shots:	# of Shots:	# of Shots:	# of Shots:
Ave Reload Time:		Ave Total Rep Time:		Notes:

FEED IT

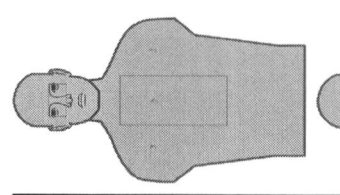 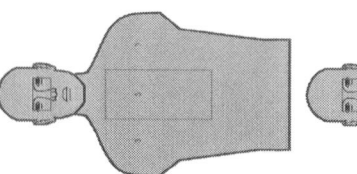 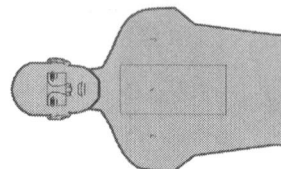

Date:	Location:	Weapon:	Sights:	A Box: Head / Body
Rep 1 Time:	Rep 2 Time:	Rep 3 Time:	Rep 4 Time:	Rep 5 Time:
Reload Time:	Reload Time:	Reload Time:	Reload Time:	Reload Time:
A Box: Go / No Go	A Box: Go / No Go	A Box: Go / No Go	A Box: Go / No Go	A Box: Go / No Go
# of Shots::	# of Shots:	# of Shots:	# of Shots:	# of Shots:
Ave Reload Time:		Ave Total Rep Time:		Notes:

Date:	Location:	Weapon:	Sights:	A Box: Head / Body
Rep 1 Time:	Rep 2 Time:	Rep 3 Time:	Rep 4 Time:	Rep 5 Time:
Reload Time:	Reload Time:	Reload Time:	Reload Time:	Reload Time:
A Box: Go / No Go	A Box: Go / No Go	A Box: Go / No Go	A Box: Go / No Go	A Box: Go / No Go
# of Shots:	# of Shots:	# of Shots:	# of Shots:	# of Shots:
Ave Reload Time:		Ave Total Rep Time:		Notes:

Date:	Location:	Weapon:	Sights:	A Box: Head / Body
Rep 1 Time:	Rep 2 Time:	Rep 3 Time:	Rep 4 Time:	Rep 5 Time:
Reload Time:	Reload Time:	Reload Time:	Reload Time:	Reload Time:
A Box: Go / No Go	A Box: Go / No Go	A Box: Go / No Go	A Box: Go / No Go	A Box: Go / No Go
# of Shots:	# of Shots:	# of Shots:	# of Shots:	# of Shots:
Ave Reload Time:		Ave Total Rep Time:		Notes:

www.GUNFIGHTERSERIES.com ©

FEED IT

Date:	Location:	Weapon:	Sights:	A Box: Head / Body
Rep 1 Time:	Rep 2 Time:	Rep 3 Time:	Rep 4 Time:	Rep 5 Time:
Reload Time:	Reload Time:	Reload Time:	Reload Time:	Reload Time:
A Box: Go / No Go	A Box: Go / No Go	A Box: Go / No Go	A Box: Go / No Go	A Box: Go / No Go
# of Shots:	# of Shots:	# of Shots:	# of Shots:	# of Shots:
Ave Reload Time:		Ave Total Rep Time:		Notes:
Date:	Location:	Weapon:	Sights:	A Box: Head / Body
Rep 1 Time:	Rep 2 Time:	Rep 3 Time:	Rep 4 Time:	Rep 5 Time:
Reload Time:	Reload Time:	Reload Time:	Reload Time:	Reload Time:
A Box: Go / No Go	A Box: Go / No Go	A Box: Go / No Go	A Box: Go / No Go	A Box: Go / No Go
# of Shots:	# of Shots:	# of Shots:	# of Shots:	# of Shots:
Ave Reload Time:		Ave Total Rep Time:		Notes:
Date:	Location:	Weapon:	Sights:	A Box: Head / Body
Rep 1 Time:	Rep 2 Time:	Rep 3 Time:	Rep 4 Time:	Rep 5 Time:
Reload Time:	Reload Time:	Reload Time:	Reload Time:	Reload Time:
A Box: Go / No Go	A Box: Go / No Go	A Box: Go / No Go	A Box: Go / No Go	A Box: Go / No Go
# of Shots::	# of Shots:	# of Shots:	# of Shots:	# of Shots:
Ave Reload Time:		Ave Total Rep Time:		Notes:

FEED IT

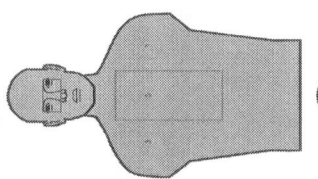
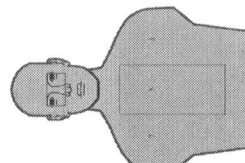

Date:	Location:	Weapon:	Sights:	A Box: Head / Body
Rep 1 Time:	Rep 2 Time:	Rep 3 Time:	Rep 4 Time:	Rep 5 Time:
Reload Time:	Reload Time:	Reload Time:	Reload Time:	Reload Time:
A Box: Go / No Go	A Box: Go / No Go	A Box: Go / No Go	A Box: Go / No Go	A Box: Go / No Go
# of Shots:	# of Shots:	# of Shots:	# of Shots:	# of Shots:
Ave Reload Time:		Ave Total Rep Time:		Notes:
Date:	Location:	Weapon:	Sights:	A Box: Head / Body
Rep 1 Time:	Rep 2 Time:	Rep 3 Time:	Rep 4 Time:	Rep 5 Time:
Reload Time:	Reload Time:	Reload Time:	Reload Time:	Reload Time:
A Box: Go / No Go	A Box: Go / No Go	A Box: Go / No Go	A Box: Go / No Go	A Box: Go / No Go
# of Shots:	# of Shots:	# of Shots:	# of Shots:	# of Shots:
Ave Reload Time:		Ave Total Rep Time:		Notes:
Date:	Location:	Weapon:	Sights:	A Box: Head / Body
Rep 1 Time:	Rep 2 Time:	Rep 3 Time:	Rep 4 Time:	Rep 5 Time:
Reload Time:	Reload Time:	Reload Time:	Reload Time:	Reload Time:
A Box: Go / No Go	A Box: Go / No Go	A Box: Go / No Go	A Box: Go / No Go	A Box: Go / No Go
# of Shots::	# of Shots:	# of Shots:	# of Shots:	# of Shots:
Ave Reload Time:		Ave Total Rep Time:		Notes:

www.GUNFIGHTERSERIES.com ©

FEED IT

Date:	Location:	Weapon:	Sights:	A Box: Head / Body
Rep 1 Time:	Rep 2 Time:	Rep 3 Time:	Rep 4 Time:	Rep 5 Time:
Reload Time:	Reload Time:	Reload Time:	Reload Time:	Reload Time:
A Box: Go / No Go	A Box: Go / No Go	A Box: Go / No Go	A Box: Go / No Go	A Box: Go / No Go
# of Shots:	# of Shots:	# of Shots:	# of Shots:	# of Shots:
Ave Reload Time:		Ave Total Rep Time:		Notes:
Date:	Location:	Weapon:	Sights:	A Box: Head / Body
Rep 1 Time:	Rep 2 Time:	Rep 3 Time:	Rep 4 Time:	Rep 5 Time:
Reload Time:	Reload Time:	Reload Time:	Reload Time:	Reload Time:
A Box: Go / No Go	A Box: Go / No Go	A Box: Go / No Go	A Box: Go / No Go	A Box: Go / No Go
# of Shots:	# of Shots:	# of Shots:	# of Shots:	# of Shots:
Ave Reload Time:		Ave Total Rep Time:		Notes:
Date:	Location:	Weapon:	Sights:	A Box: Head / Body
Rep 1 Time:	Rep 2 Time:	Rep 3 Time:	Rep 4 Time:	Rep 5 Time:
Reload Time:	Reload Time:	Reload Time:	Reload Time:	Reload Time:
A Box: Go / No Go	A Box: Go / No Go	A Box: Go / No Go	A Box: Go / No Go	A Box: Go / No Go
# of Shots::	# of Shots:	# of Shots:	# of Shots:	# of Shots:
Ave Reload Time:		Ave Total Rep Time:		Notes:

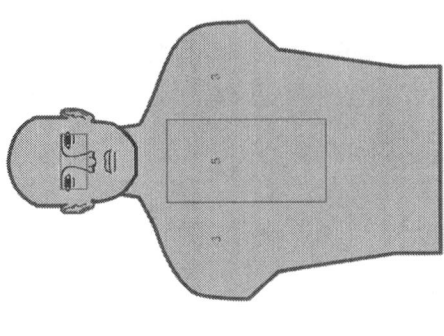

CARBINE PUSH PULL…

Purpose: Increase type 1 malfunction clearance speed and recoil management.

Distance: 25 Yards.

Target: JD-QUAL1

Par Time: 4 Seconds.

Extra Equipment Needed: Shot timer.

Rounds Fired Per Rep: 2 to 5 Rounds.

Point Penalty: Go / No Go.

Repetitions: 5 Reps.

Total Rounds Fired: 10 to 25 Rounds.

Starting Position & Condition: Carbine pointed at target. Condition 3, weapon cocked. This weapon condition will simulate a Type 1 malfunction condition.

Description: At the timer beep, press the trigger and attempt to fire. Hearing the click, grab the magazine and push it up to see if it's seated, then pull the magazine down to make sure it locked into the magazine well. Rack the charging handle chambering a new round, aim and fire 2 to 5 rounds into the (5 point) A Zone body box. Record the time. Repeat 4 more times firing the same number of rounds after clearing the malfunction as the previous repetitions. Remove the high and low times and average the 3 remaining times for an average. Try different round counts on different sessions and over time, see if your average times for the same round counts are coming down.

Goals: Novice: 5 Seconds.   Expert: 3.5 Seconds.   Gunfighter: 2.5 Seconds.

CARBINE PUSH PULL...

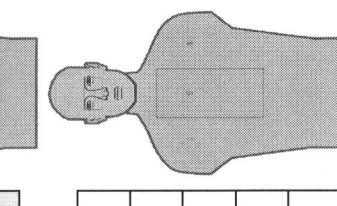

Date:	Location:	Weapon:	Sights:	A Box: Head / Body
Rep 1 Time:	Rep 2 Time:	Rep 3 Time:	Rep 4 Time:	Rep 5 Time:
A Box: Go / No Go	A Box: Go / No Go	A Box: Go / No Go	A Box: Go / No Go	A Box: Go / No Go
# of Shots:	# of Shots:	# of Shots:	# of Shots:	# of Shots:
Notes:			Ave Total Rep Time:	

Date:	Location:	Weapon:	Sights:	A Box: Head / Body
Rep 1 Time:	Rep 2 Time:	Rep 3 Time:	Rep 4 Time:	Rep 5 Time:
A Box: Go / No Go	A Box: Go / No Go	A Box: Go / No Go	A Box: Go / No Go	A Box: Go / No Go
# of Shots:	# of Shots:	# of Shots:	# of Shots:	# of Shots:
Notes:			Ave Total Rep Time:	

Date:	Location:	Weapon:	Sights:	A Box: Head / Body
Rep 1 Time:	Rep 2 Time:	Rep 3 Time:	Rep 4 Time:	Rep 5 Time:
A Box: Go / No Go	A Box: Go / No Go	A Box: Go / No Go	A Box: Go / No Go	A Box: Go / No Go
# of Shots:	# of Shots:	# of Shots:	# of Shots:	# of Shots:
Notes:			Ave Total Rep Time:	

Manipulation Drills - 4

Fundamental Carbine ©

CARBINE PUSH PULL...

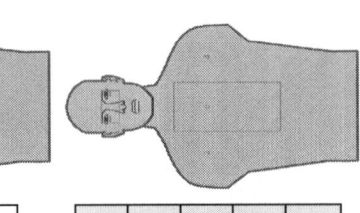
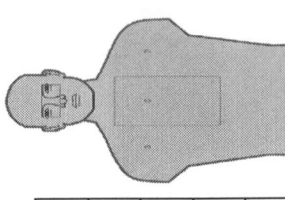

Date:	Location:	Weapon:	Sights:	A Box: Head / Body
Rep 1 Time:	Rep 2 Time:	Rep 3 Time:	Rep 4 Time:	Rep 5 Time:
A Box: Go / No Go	A Box: Go / No Go	A Box: Go / No Go	A Box: Go / No Go	A Box: Go / No Go
# of Shots:	# of Shots:	# of Shots:	# of Shots:	# of Shots:
Notes:			Ave Total Rep Time:	

Date:	Location:	Weapon:	Sights:	A Box: Head / Body
Rep 1 Time:	Rep 2 Time:	Rep 3 Time:	Rep 4 Time:	Rep 5 Time:
A Box: Go / No Go	A Box: Go / No Go	A Box: Go / No Go	A Box: Go / No Go	A Box: Go / No Go
# of Shots:	# of Shots:	# of Shots:	# of Shots:	# of Shots:
Notes:			Ave Total Rep Time:	

Date:	Location:	Weapon:	Sights:	A Box: Head / Body
Rep 1 Time:	Rep 2 Time:	Rep 3 Time:	Rep 4 Time:	Rep 5 Time:
A Box: Go / No Go	A Box: Go / No Go	A Box: Go / No Go	A Box: Go / No Go	A Box: Go / No Go
# of Shots:	# of Shots:	# of Shots:	# of Shots:	# of Shots:
Notes:			Ave Total Rep Time:	

www.GUNFIGHTERSERIES.com ©

CARBINE PUSH PULL...

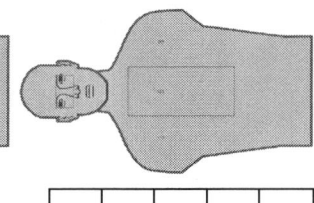

Date:	Location:	Weapon:	Sights:	A Box: Head / Body
Rep 1 Time:	Rep 2 Time:	Rep 3 Time:	Rep 4 Time:	Rep 5 Time:
A Box: Go / No Go	A Box: Go / No Go	A Box: Go / No Go	A Box: Go / No Go	A Box: Go / No Go
# of Shots:	# of Shots:	# of Shots:	# of Shots:	# of Shots:
Notes:			Ave Total Rep Time:	

Date:	Location:	Weapon:	Sights:	A Box: Head / Body
Rep 1 Time:	Rep 2 Time:	Rep 3 Time:	Rep 4 Time:	Rep 5 Time:
A Box: Go / No Go	A Box: Go / No Go	A Box: Go / No Go	A Box: Go / No Go	A Box: Go / No Go
# of Shots:	# of Shots:	# of Shots:	# of Shots:	# of Shots:
Notes:			Ave Total Rep Time:	

Date:	Location:	Weapon:	Sights:	A Box: Head / Body
Rep 1 Time:	Rep 2 Time:	Rep 3 Time:	Rep 4 Time:	Rep 5 Time:
A Box: Go / No Go	A Box: Go / No Go	A Box: Go / No Go	A Box: Go / No Go	A Box: Go / No Go
# of Shots:	# of Shots:	# of Shots:	# of Shots:	# of Shots:
Notes:			Ave Total Rep Time:	

Manipulation Drills - 4

Fundamental Carbine ©

CARBINE PUSH PULL...

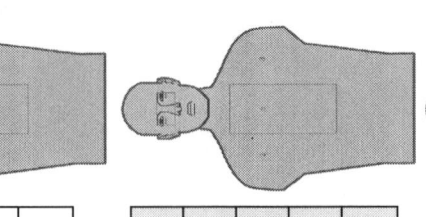
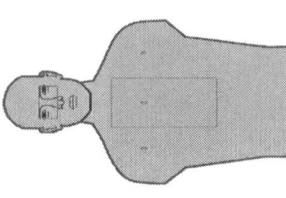

Date:	Location:	Weapon:	Sights:	A Box: Head / Body
Rep 1 Time:	Rep 2 Time:	Rep 3 Time:	Rep 4 Time:	Rep 5 Time:
A Box: Go / No Go	A Box: Go / No Go	A Box: Go / No Go	A Box: Go / No Go	A Box: Go / No Go
# of Shots:	# of Shots:	# of Shots:	# of Shots:	# of Shots:
Notes:			Ave Total Rep Time:	

Date:	Location:	Weapon:	Sights:	A Box: Head / Body
Rep 1 Time:	Rep 2 Time:	Rep 3 Time:	Rep 4 Time:	Rep 5 Time:
A Box: Go / No Go	A Box: Go / No Go	A Box: Go / No Go	A Box: Go / No Go	A Box: Go / No Go
# of Shots:	# of Shots:	# of Shots:	# of Shots:	# of Shots:
Notes:			Ave Total Rep Time:	

Date:	Location:	Weapon:	Sights:	A Box: Head / Body
Rep 1 Time:	Rep 2 Time:	Rep 3 Time:	Rep 4 Time:	Rep 5 Time:
A Box: Go / No Go	A Box: Go / No Go	A Box: Go / No Go	A Box: Go / No Go	A Box: Go / No Go
# of Shots:	# of Shots:	# of Shots:	# of Shots:	# of Shots:
Notes:			Ave Total Rep Time:	

www.GUNFIGHTERSERIES.com ©

CARBINE PUSH PULL...

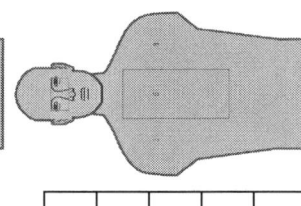

Date:	Location:	Weapon:	Sights:	A Box: Head / Body
Rep 1 Time:	Rep 2 Time:	Rep 3 Time:	Rep 4 Time:	Rep 5 Time:
A Box: Go / No Go	A Box: Go / No Go	A Box: Go / No Go	A Box: Go / No Go	A Box: Go / No Go
# of Shots:	# of Shots:	# of Shots:	# of Shots:	# of Shots:
Notes:			Ave Total Rep Time:	

Date:	Location:	Weapon:	Sights:	A Box: Head / Body
Rep 1 Time:	Rep 2 Time:	Rep 3 Time:	Rep 4 Time:	Rep 5 Time:
A Box: Go / No Go	A Box: Go / No Go	A Box: Go / No Go	A Box: Go / No Go	A Box: Go / No Go
# of Shots:	# of Shots:	# of Shots:	# of Shots:	# of Shots:
Notes:			Ave Total Rep Time:	

Date:	Location:	Weapon:	Sights:	A Box: Head / Body
Rep 1 Time:	Rep 2 Time:	Rep 3 Time:	Rep 4 Time:	Rep 5 Time:
A Box: Go / No Go	A Box: Go / No Go	A Box: Go / No Go	A Box: Go / No Go	A Box: Go / No Go
# of Shots:	# of Shots:	# of Shots:	# of Shots:	# of Shots:
Notes:			Ave Total Rep Time:	

Manipulation Drills - 4

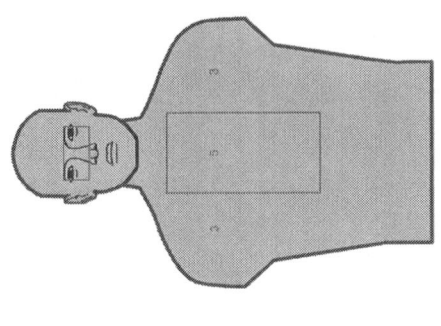

CARBINE DUBLIN

Purpose: Increase type 2 malfunction clearance speed and recoil management.

Distance: 25 Yards.

Target: JD-QUAL1

Extra Equipment Needed: Shot timer, 2 magazines and 1 magazine pouch.

Rounds Fired Per Rep: 2 to 5 Rounds. **Total Rounds Fired:** 10 to 25 Rounds.

Point Penalty: Go / No Go.

Repetitions: 5 Reps.

Starting Position & Condition: Standing - Carbine pointed at target. Condition 3 with carbine put in a Type 2 (double feed) malfunction condition.

Description: At the timer beep, press the trigger and attempt to fire. Hearing no click and feeling a mushy trigger: tilt the carbine and observe the chamber. Upon seeing the double feed, rack the charging handle and lock the bolt carrier back. Remove the magazine and let it drop to the ground. Rack the charging handle 3 times or until you see the stuck round/case in the chamber extracted. Bring the magazine well up in front of your face with the pistol grip just below your eyes, so you can maintain situational awareness. Lock the butt stock into your side with your elbow tucked into your side, take a magazine out of your magazine pouch with live rounds in it and insert it into the magazine well. Push the magazine forcefully to the point where you hear a click of the magazine being locked in place. Rack the charging handle to chamber a round, aim and fire 2 to 5 rounds into the A Zone (5 point) body box after loading. Record the time. Repeat 4 more times firing the same number of rounds after clearing the malfunction as the previous repetitions. Remove the high and low times and average the 3 remaining times for an average. Try different round counts on different sessions and over time, see if your average times for the same round counts are coming down.

Goals: To be smooth and deliberate.

CARBINE DUBLIN

Date:	Location:	Weapon:	Sights:	A Box: Head / Body
Rep 1 Time:	Rep 2 Time:	Rep 3 Time:	Rep 4 Time:	Rep 5 Time:
1st Shot Time:	1st Shot Time:	1st Shot Time:	1st Shot Time:	1st Shot Time:
A Box: Go / No Go	A Box: Go / No Go	A Box: Go / No Go	A Box: Go / No Go	A Box: Go / No Go
# of Shots:	# of Shots:	# of Shots:	# of Shots:	# of Shots:
Ave 1st Shot Time:		Ave Total Rep Time:		Notes:

Date:	Location:	Weapon:	Sights:	A Box: Head / Body
Rep 1 Time:	Rep 2 Time:	Rep 3 Time:	Rep 4 Time:	Rep 5 Time:
1st Shot Time:	1st Shot Time:	1st Shot Time:	1st Shot Time:	1st Shot Time:
A Box: Go / No Go	A Box: Go / No Go	A Box: Go / No Go	A Box: Go / No Go	A Box: Go / No Go
# of Shots:	# of Shots:	# of Shots:	# of Shots:	# of Shots:
Ave 1st Shot Time:		Ave Total Rep Time:		Notes:

Date:	Location:	Weapon:	Sights:	A Box: Head / Body
Rep 1 Time:	Rep 2 Time:	Rep 3 Time:	Rep 4 Time:	Rep 5 Time:
1st Shot Time:	1st Shot Time:	1st Shot Time:	1st Shot Time:	1st Shot Time:
A Box: Go / No Go	A Box: Go / No Go	A Box: Go / No Go	A Box: Go / No Go	A Box: Go / No Go
# of Shots:	# of Shots:	# of Shots:	# of Shots:	# of Shots:
Ave 1st Shot Time:		Ave Total Rep Time:		Notes:

CARBINE DUBLIN

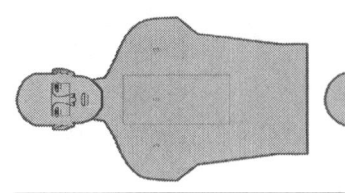
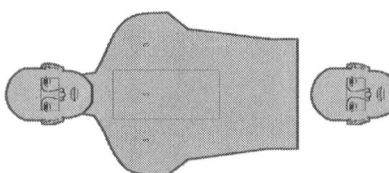
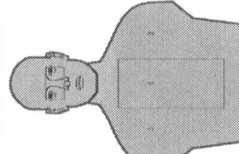

Date:	Location:	Weapon:	Sights:	A Box: Head / Body
Rep 1 Time:	Rep 2 Time:	Rep 3 Time:	Rep 4 Time:	Rep 5 Time:
1st Shot Time:	1st Shot Time:	1st Shot Time:	1st Shot Time:	1st Shot Time:
A Box: Go / No Go	A Box: Go / No Go	A Box: Go / No Go	A Box: Go / No Go	A Box: Go / No Go
# of Shots:	# of Shots:	# of Shots:	# of Shots:	# of Shots:
Ave 1st Shot Time:		Ave Total Rep Time:		Notes:
Date:	Location:	Weapon:	Sights:	A Box: Head / Body
Rep 1 Time:	Rep 2 Time:	Rep 3 Time:	Rep 4 Time:	Rep 5 Time:
1st Shot Time:	1st Shot Time:	1st Shot Time:	1st Shot Time:	1st Shot Time:
A Box: Go / No Go	A Box: Go / No Go	A Box: Go / No Go	A Box: Go / No Go	A Box: Go / No Go
# of Shots:	# of Shots:	# of Shots:	# of Shots:	# of Shots:
Ave 1st Shot Time:		Ave Total Rep Time:		Notes:
Date:	Location:	Weapon:	Sights:	A Box: Head / Body
Rep 1 Time:	Rep 2 Time:	Rep 3 Time:	Rep 4 Time:	Rep 5 Time:
1st Shot Time:	1st Shot Time:	1st Shot Time:	1st Shot Time:	1st Shot Time:
A Box: Go / No Go	A Box: Go / No Go	A Box: Go / No Go	A Box: Go / No Go	A Box: Go / No Go
# of Shots:	# of Shots:	# of Shots:	# of Shots:	# of Shots:
Ave 1st Shot Time:		Ave Total Rep Time:		Notes:

www.GUNFIGHTERSERIES.com ©

CARBINE DUBLIN

Date:	Location:	Weapon:	Sights:	A Box: Head / Body
Rep 1 Time:	Rep 2 Time:	Rep 3 Time:	Rep 4 Time:	Rep 5 Time:
1st Shot Time:	1st Shot Time:	1st Shot Time:	1st Shot Time:	1st Shot Time:
A Box: Go / No Go	A Box: Go / No Go	A Box: Go / No Go	A Box: Go / No Go	A Box: Go / No Go
# of Shots:	# of Shots:	# of Shots:	# of Shots:	# of Shots:
Ave 1st Shot Time:		Ave Total Rep Time:		Notes:

Date:	Location:	Weapon:	Sights:	A Box: Head / Body
Rep 1 Time:	Rep 2 Time:	Rep 3 Time:	Rep 4 Time:	Rep 5 Time:
1st Shot Time:	1st Shot Time:	1st Shot Time:	1st Shot Time:	1st Shot Time:
A Box: Go / No Go	A Box: Go / No Go	A Box: Go / No Go	A Box: Go / No Go	A Box: Go / No Go
# of Shots:	# of Shots:	# of Shots:	# of Shots:	# of Shots:
Ave 1st Shot Time:		Ave Total Rep Time:		Notes:

Date:	Location:	Weapon:	Sights:	A Box: Head / Body
Rep 1 Time:	Rep 2 Time:	Rep 3 Time:	Rep 4 Time:	Rep 5 Time:
1st Shot Time:	1st Shot Time:	1st Shot Time:	1st Shot Time:	1st Shot Time:
A Box: Go / No Go	A Box: Go / No Go	A Box: Go / No Go	A Box: Go / No Go	A Box: Go / No Go
# of Shots:	# of Shots:	# of Shots:	# of Shots:	# of Shots:
Ave 1st Shot Time:		Ave Total Rep Time:		Notes:

CARBINE DUBLIN

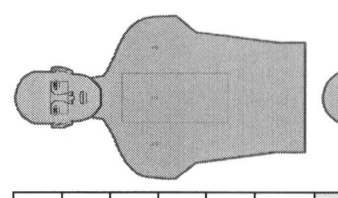 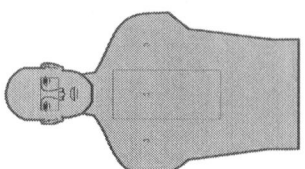 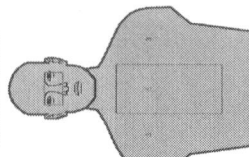

Date:	Location:	Weapon:	Sights:	A Box: Head / Body
Rep 1 Time:	Rep 2 Time:	Rep 3 Time:	Rep 4 Time:	Rep 5 Time:
1st Shot Time:	1st Shot Time:	1st Shot Time:	1st Shot Time:	1st Shot Time:
A Box: Go / No Go	A Box: Go / No Go	A Box: Go / No Go	A Box: Go / No Go	A Box: Go / No Go
# of Shots:	# of Shots:	# of Shots:	# of Shots:	# of Shots:
Ave 1st Shot Time:		Ave Total Rep Time:		Notes:
Date:	Location:	Weapon:	Sights:	A Box: Head / Body
Rep 1 Time:	Rep 2 Time:	Rep 3 Time:	Rep 4 Time:	Rep 5 Time:
1st Shot Time:	1st Shot Time:	1st Shot Time:	1st Shot Time:	1st Shot Time:
A Box: Go / No Go	A Box: Go / No Go	A Box: Go / No Go	A Box: Go / No Go	A Box: Go / No Go
# of Shots:	# of Shots:	# of Shots:	# of Shots:	# of Shots:
Ave 1st Shot Time:		Ave Total Rep Time:		Notes:
Date:	Location:	Weapon:	Sights:	A Box: Head / Body
Rep 1 Time:	Rep 2 Time:	Rep 3 Time:	Rep 4 Time:	Rep 5 Time:
1st Shot Time:	1st Shot Time:	1st Shot Time:	1st Shot Time:	1st Shot Time:
A Box: Go / No Go	A Box: Go / No Go	A Box: Go / No Go	A Box: Go / No Go	A Box: Go / No Go
# of Shots:	# of Shots:	# of Shots:	# of Shots:	# of Shots:
Ave 1st Shot Time:		Ave Total Rep Time:		Notes:

www.GUNFIGHTERSERIES.com ©

CARBINE DUBLIN

Date:	Location:	Weapon:	Sights:	A Box: Head / Body
Rep 1 Time:	Rep 2 Time:	Rep 3 Time:	Rep 4 Time:	Rep 5 Time:
1st Shot Time:	1st Shot Time:	1st Shot Time:	1st Shot Time:	1st Shot Time:
A Box: Go / No Go	A Box: Go / No Go	A Box: Go / No Go	A Box: Go / No Go	A Box: Go / No Go
# of Shots:	# of Shots:	# of Shots:	# of Shots:	# of Shots:
Ave 1st Shot Time:		Ave Total Rep Time:		Notes:

Date:	Location:	Weapon:	Sights:	A Box: Head / Body
Rep 1 Time:	Rep 2 Time:	Rep 3 Time:	Rep 4 Time:	Rep 5 Time:
1st Shot Time:	1st Shot Time:	1st Shot Time:	1st Shot Time:	1st Shot Time:
A Box: Go / No Go	A Box: Go / No Go	A Box: Go / No Go	A Box: Go / No Go	A Box: Go / No Go
# of Shots:	# of Shots:	# of Shots:	# of Shots:	# of Shots:
Ave 1st Shot Time:		Ave Total Rep Time:		Notes:

Date:	Location:	Weapon:	Sights:	A Box: Head / Body
Rep 1 Time:	Rep 2 Time:	Rep 3 Time:	Rep 4 Time:	Rep 5 Time:
1st Shot Time:	1st Shot Time:	1st Shot Time:	1st Shot Time:	1st Shot Time:
A Box: Go / No Go	A Box: Go / No Go	A Box: Go / No Go	A Box: Go / No Go	A Box: Go / No Go
# of Shots:	# of Shots:	# of Shots:	# of Shots:	# of Shots:
Ave 1st Shot Time:		Ave Total Rep Time:		Notes:

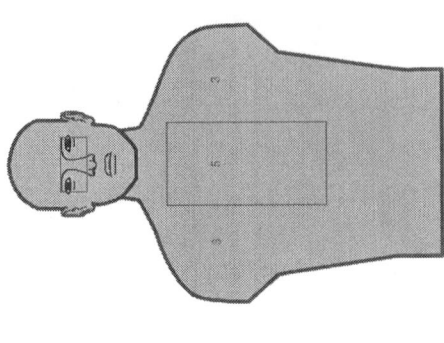

10 x 5

Purpose: Increase reloading speed, nervous system memory of an emergency reload and recoil management.

Distance: 10 Yards.

Target: JD-QUAL1

Par Time: 6 Seconds.

Extra Equipment Needed: Shot timer, 2 magazines and 1 magazine pouch.

Rounds Fired Per Rep: 5 Rounds.   **Total Rounds Fired:** 25 Rounds.

Point Penalty: Go / No Go.

Repetitions: 5 Reps.

Starting Position & Condition: Standing - Carbine pointed at target. Condition 1 with a magazine with 1 round in it.

Description: Carbine pointed at target, at the timer beep, fire 2 rounds, perform an emergency reload, aim and fire 3 rounds into the (5 point) A Zone body box after reloading. Record the time. Repeat 4 more times. Record your results for reference. Left handed shooters add .5 seconds. From vest mag pouches add .5 seconds to par time.

Goals: Novice: 6 Seconds.   Expert: 5 Seconds.   Gunfighter: 4 Seconds.

10 X 5

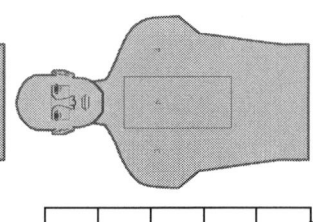

Date:	Location:	Weapon:	Sights:	A Box: Head / Body
Rep 1 Time:	Rep 2 Time:	Rep 3 Time:	Rep 4 Time:	Rep 5 Time:
Reload Time:	Reload Time:	Reload Time:	Reload Time:	Reload Time:
Rep 1: Go / No Go	Rep 2: Go / No Go	Rep 3: Go / No Go	Rep 4: Go / No Go	Rep 5: Go / No Go
Total Rep Score:		Notes:		

Date:	Location:	Weapon:	Sights:	A Box: Head / Body
Rep 1 Time:	Rep 2 Time:	Rep 3 Time:	Rep 4 Time:	Rep 5 Time:
Reload Time:	Reload Time:	Reload Time:	Reload Time:	Reload Time:
Rep 1: Go / No Go	Rep 2: Go / No Go	Rep 3: Go / No Go	Rep 4: Go / No Go	Rep 5: Go / No Go
Total Rep Score:		Notes:		

Date:	Location:	Weapon:	Sights:	A Box: Head / Body
Rep 1 Time:	Rep 2 Time:	Rep 3 Time:	Rep 4 Time:	Rep 5 Time:
Reload Time:	Reload Time:	Reload Time:	Reload Time:	Reload Time:
Rep 1: Go / No Go	Rep 2: Go / No Go	Rep 3: Go / No Go	Rep 4: Go / No Go	Rep 5: Go / No Go
Total Rep Score:		Notes:		

Fundamental Carbine ©

Manipulation Drills - 6

10 X 5

Date:	Location:	Weapon:	Sights:	A Box: Head / Body
Rep 1 Time:	Rep 2 Time:	Rep 3 Time:	Rep 4 Time:	Rep 5 Time:
Reload Time:	Reload Time:	Reload Time:	Reload Time:	Reload Time:
Rep 1: Go / No Go	Rep 2: Go / No Go	Rep 3: Go / No Go	Rep 4: Go / No Go	Rep 5: Go / No Go
Total Rep Score:		Notes:		

Date:	Location:	Weapon:	Sights:	A Box: Head / Body
Rep 1 Time:	Rep 2 Time:	Rep 3 Time:	Rep 4 Time:	Rep 5 Time:
Reload Time:	Reload Time:	Reload Time:	Reload Time:	Reload Time:
Rep 1: Go / No Go	Rep 2: Go / No Go	Rep 3: Go / No Go	Rep 4: Go / No Go	Rep 5: Go / No Go
Total Rep Score:		Notes:		

Date:	Location:	Weapon:	Sights:	A Box: Head / Body
Rep 1 Time:	Rep 2 Time:	Rep 3 Time:	Rep 4 Time:	Rep 5 Time:
Reload Time:	Reload Time:	Reload Time:	Reload Time:	Reload Time:
Rep 1: Go / No Go	Rep 2: Go / No Go	Rep 3: Go / No Go	Rep 4: Go / No Go	Rep 5: Go / No Go
Total Rep Score:		Notes:		

www.GUNFIGHTERSERIES.com ©

10 X 5

Date:	Location:	Weapon:	Sights:	A Box: Head / Body
Rep 1 Time:	Rep 2 Time:	Rep 3 Time:	Rep 4 Time:	Rep 5 Time:
Reload Time:	Reload Time:	Reload Time:	Reload Time:	Reload Time:
Rep 1: Go / No Go	Rep 2: Go / No Go	Rep 3: Go / No Go	Rep 4: Go / No Go	Rep 5: Go / No Go
Total Rep Score:		Notes:		

Date:	Location:	Weapon:	Sights:	A Box: Head / Body
Rep 1 Time:	Rep 2 Time:	Rep 3 Time:	Rep 4 Time:	Rep 5 Time:
Reload Time:	Reload Time:	Reload Time:	Reload Time:	Reload Time:
Rep 1: Go / No Go	Rep 2: Go / No Go	Rep 3: Go / No Go	Rep 4: Go / No Go	Rep 5: Go / No Go
Total Rep Score:		Notes:		

Date:	Location:	Weapon:	Sights:	A Box: Head / Body
Rep 1 Time:	Rep 2 Time:	Rep 3 Time:	Rep 4 Time:	Rep 5 Time:
Reload Time:	Reload Time:	Reload Time:	Reload Time:	Reload Time:
Rep 1: Go / No Go	Rep 2: Go / No Go	Rep 3: Go / No Go	Rep 4: Go / No Go	Rep 5: Go / No Go
Total Rep Score:		Notes:		

Fundamental Carbine © — Manipulation Drills - 6

10 X 5

Date:	Location:	Weapon:	Sights:	A Box: Head / Body
Rep 1 Time:	Rep 2 Time:	Rep 3 Time:	Rep 4 Time:	Rep 5 Time:
Reload Time:	Reload Time:	Reload Time:	Reload Time:	Reload Time:
Rep 1: Go / No Go	Rep 2: Go / No Go	Rep 3: Go / No Go	Rep 4: Go / No Go	Rep 5: Go / No Go
Total Rep Score:		Notes:		

Date:	Location:	Weapon:	Sights:	A Box: Head / Body
Rep 1 Time:	Rep 2 Time:	Rep 3 Time:	Rep 4 Time:	Rep 5 Time:
Reload Time:	Reload Time:	Reload Time:	Reload Time:	Reload Time:
Rep 1: Go / No Go	Rep 2: Go / No Go	Rep 3: Go / No Go	Rep 4: Go / No Go	Rep 5: Go / No Go
Total Rep Score:		Notes:		

Date:	Location:	Weapon:	Sights:	A Box: Head / Body
Rep 1 Time:	Rep 2 Time:	Rep 3 Time:	Rep 4 Time:	Rep 5 Time:
Reload Time:	Reload Time:	Reload Time:	Reload Time:	Reload Time:
Rep 1: Go / No Go	Rep 2: Go / No Go	Rep 3: Go / No Go	Rep 4: Go / No Go	Rep 5: Go / No Go
Total Rep Score:		Notes:		

www.GUNFIGHTERSERIES.com ©

10 X 5

Date:	Location:	Weapon:	Sights:	A Box: Head / Body
Rep 1 Time:	Rep 2 Time:	Rep 3 Time:	Rep 4 Time:	Rep 5 Time:
Reload Time:	Reload Time:	Reload Time:	Reload Time:	Reload Time:
Rep 1: Go / No Go	Rep 2: Go / No Go	Rep 3: Go / No Go	Rep 4: Go / No Go	Rep 5: Go / No Go
Total Rep Score:		Notes:		

Date:	Location:	Weapon:	Sights:	A Box: Head / Body
Rep 1 Time:	Rep 2 Time:	Rep 3 Time:	Rep 4 Time:	Rep 5 Time:
Reload Time:	Reload Time:	Reload Time:	Reload Time:	Reload Time:
Rep 1: Go / No Go	Rep 2: Go / No Go	Rep 3: Go / No Go	Rep 4: Go / No Go	Rep 5: Go / No Go
Total Rep Score:		Notes:		

Date:	Location:	Weapon:	Sights:	A Box: Head / Body
Rep 1 Time:	Rep 2 Time:	Rep 3 Time:	Rep 4 Time:	Rep 5 Time:
Reload Time:	Reload Time:	Reload Time:	Reload Time:	Reload Time:
Rep 1: Go / No Go	Rep 2: Go / No Go	Rep 3: Go / No Go	Rep 4: Go / No Go	Rep 5: Go / No Go
Total Rep Score:		Notes:		

Fundamental Carbine ©

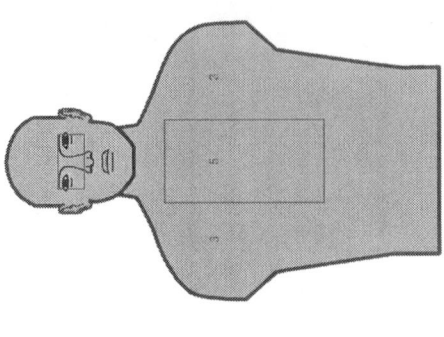

GO TO GUN

Purpose: Increase weapon transition speed, nervous system memory of a transition to pistol and recoil management.

Distance: 10 Yards.

Target: JD-QUAL1

Par Time: 5 Seconds.

Extra Equipment Needed: Shot timer, pistol holster and carbine with sling.

Rounds Fired Per Rep: 5 Rounds. (2 Carbine & 3 Pistol)   **Total Rounds Fired:** 25 Rounds. (10 Carbine & 15 Pistol)

Point Penalty: Go / No Go.

Repetitions: 5 Reps.

Starting Position & Condition: Standing - Pistol condition 1 and holstered. Carbine pointed at target. Condition 1 with a magazine with 1 round in it.

Description: At the timer beep, fire 2 rounds, perform a transition to pistol, aim and fire 3 rounds into the (5 point) A Zone body box after transitioning. Record the time. Repeat 4 more times. Record your results for reference.

Goals: Novice: 5 Seconds.   Expert: 4.25 Seconds.   Gunfighter: 3.5 Seconds.

GO TO GUN

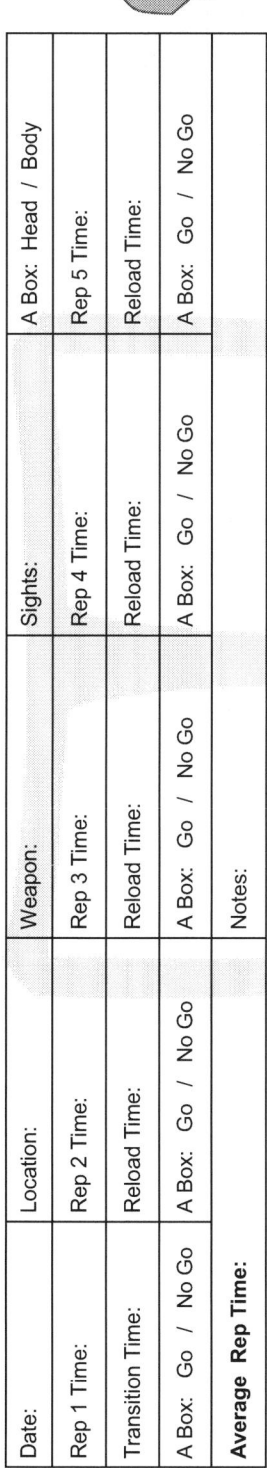

Date:	Location:	Weapon:	Sights:	A Box: Head / Body
Rep 1 Time:	Rep 2 Time:	Rep 3 Time:	Rep 4 Time:	Rep 5 Time:
Transition Time:	Reload Time:	Reload Time:	Reload Time:	Reload Time:
A Box: Go / No Go	A Box: Go / No Go	A Box: Go / No Go	A Box: Go / No Go	A Box: Go / No Go
Average Rep Time:		Notes:		

Date:	Location:	Weapon:	Sights:	A Box: Head / Body
Rep 1 Time:	Rep 2 Time:	Rep 3 Time:	Rep 4 Time:	Rep 5 Time:
Transition Time:	Reload Time:	Reload Time:	Reload Time:	Reload Time:
A Box: Go / No Go	A Box: Go / No Go	A Box: Go / No Go	A Box: Go / No Go	A Box: Go / No Go
Average Rep Time:		Notes:		

Date:	Location:	Weapon:	Sights:	A Box: Head / Body
Rep 1 Time:	Rep 2 Time:	Rep 3 Time:	Rep 4 Time:	Rep 5 Time:
Transition Time:	Reload Time:	Reload Time:	Reload Time:	Reload Time:
A Box: Go / No Go	A Box: Go / No Go	A Box: Go / No Go	A Box: Go / No Go	A Box: Go / No Go
Average Rep Time:		Notes:		

GO TO GUN

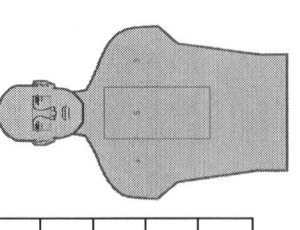

Date:	Location:	Weapon:	Sights:	A Box: Head / Body
Rep 1 Time:	Rep 2 Time:	Rep 3 Time:	Rep 4 Time:	Rep 5 Time:
Transition Time:	Reload Time:	Reload Time:	Reload Time:	Reload Time:
A Box: Go / No Go	A Box: Go / No Go	A Box: Go / No Go	A Box: Go / No Go	A Box: Go / No Go
Average Rep Time:		Notes:		

Date:	Location:	Weapon:	Sights:	A Box: Head / Body
Rep 1 Time:	Rep 2 Time:	Rep 3 Time:	Rep 4 Time:	Rep 5 Time:
Transition Time:	Reload Time:	Reload Time:	Reload Time:	Reload Time:
A Box: Go / No Go	A Box: Go / No Go	A Box: Go / No Go	A Box: Go / No Go	A Box: Go / No Go
Average Rep Time:		Notes:		

Date:	Location:	Weapon:	Sights:	A Box: Head / Body
Rep 1 Time:	Rep 2 Time:	Rep 3 Time:	Rep 4 Time:	Rep 5 Time:
Transition Time:	Reload Time:	Reload Time:	Reload Time:	Reload Time:
A Box: Go / No Go	A Box: Go / No Go	A Box: Go / No Go	A Box: Go / No Go	A Box: Go / No Go
Average Rep Time:		Notes:		

GO TO GUN

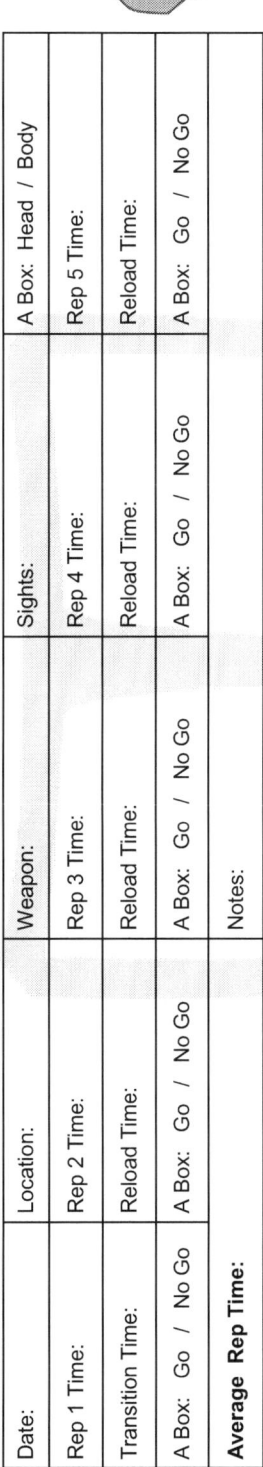

Date:	Location:	Weapon:	Sights:	A Box: Head / Body
Rep 1 Time:	Rep 2 Time:	Rep 3 Time:	Rep 4 Time:	Rep 5 Time:
Transition Time:	Reload Time:	Reload Time:	Reload Time:	Reload Time:
A Box: Go / No Go	A Box: Go / No Go	A Box: Go / No Go	A Box: Go / No Go	A Box: Go / No Go
Average Rep Time:		Notes:		

Date:	Location:	Weapon:	Sights:	A Box: Head / Body
Rep 1 Time:	Rep 2 Time:	Rep 3 Time:	Rep 4 Time:	Rep 5 Time:
Transition Time:	Reload Time:	Reload Time:	Reload Time:	Reload Time:
A Box: Go / No Go	A Box: Go / No Go	A Box: Go / No Go	A Box: Go / No Go	A Box: Go / No Go
Average Rep Time:		Notes:		

Date:	Location:	Weapon:	Sights:	A Box: Head / Body
Rep 1 Time:	Rep 2 Time:	Rep 3 Time:	Rep 4 Time:	Rep 5 Time:
Transition Time:	Reload Time:	Reload Time:	Reload Time:	Reload Time:
A Box: Go / No Go	A Box: Go / No Go	A Box: Go / No Go	A Box: Go / No Go	A Box: Go / No Go
Average Rep Time:		Notes:		

GO TO GUN

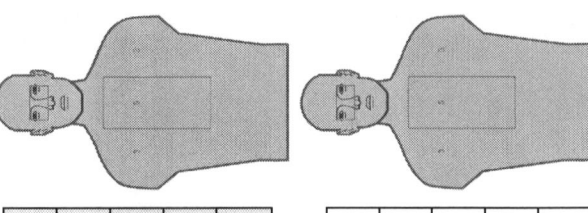

Date:	Location:	Weapon:	Sights:	A Box: Head / Body
Rep 1 Time:	Rep 2 Time:	Rep 3 Time:	Rep 4 Time:	Rep 5 Time:
Transition Time:	Reload Time:	Reload Time:	Reload Time:	Reload Time:
A Box: Go / No Go	A Box: Go / No Go	A Box: Go / No Go	A Box: Go / No Go	A Box: Go / No Go
Average Rep Time:		Notes:		

Date:	Location:	Weapon:	Sights:	A Box: Head / Body
Rep 1 Time:	Rep 2 Time:	Rep 3 Time:	Rep 4 Time:	Rep 5 Time:
Transition Time:	Reload Time:	Reload Time:	Reload Time:	Reload Time:
A Box: Go / No Go	A Box: Go / No Go	A Box: Go / No Go	A Box: Go / No Go	A Box: Go / No Go
Average Rep Time:		Notes:		

Date:	Location:	Weapon:	Sights:	A Box: Head / Body
Rep 1 Time:	Rep 2 Time:	Rep 3 Time:	Rep 4 Time:	Rep 5 Time:
Transition Time:	Reload Time:	Reload Time:	Reload Time:	Reload Time:
A Box: Go / No Go	A Box: Go / No Go	A Box: Go / No Go	A Box: Go / No Go	A Box: Go / No Go
Average Rep Time:		Notes:		

www.GUNFIGHTERSERIES.com ©

GO TO GUN

Date:	Location:	Weapon:	Sights:	A Box: Head / Body
Rep 1 Time:	Rep 2 Time:	Rep 3 Time:	Rep 4 Time:	Rep 5 Time:
Transition Time:	Reload Time:	Reload Time:	Reload Time:	Reload Time:
A Box: Go / No Go	A Box: Go / No Go	A Box: Go / No Go	A Box: Go / No Go	A Box: Go / No Go
Average Rep Time:		Notes:		

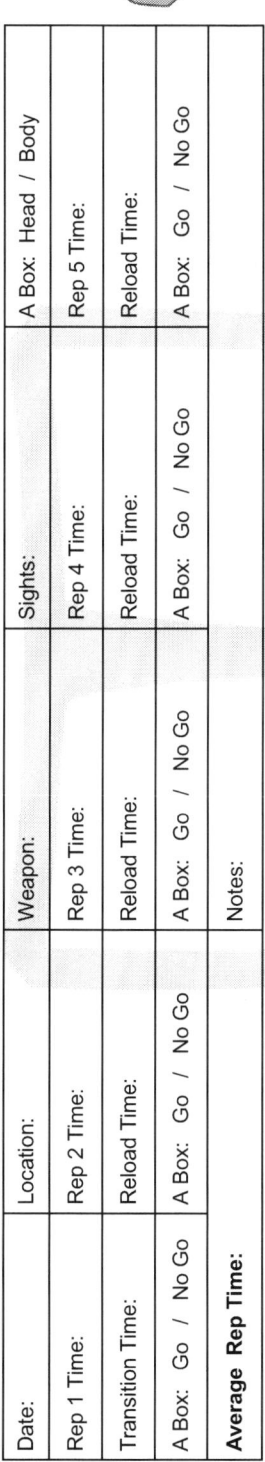

Date:	Location:	Weapon:	Sights:	A Box: Head / Body
Rep 1 Time:	Rep 2 Time:	Rep 3 Time:	Rep 4 Time:	Rep 5 Time:
Transition Time:	Reload Time:	Reload Time:	Reload Time:	Reload Time:
A Box: Go / No Go	A Box: Go / No Go	A Box: Go / No Go	A Box: Go / No Go	A Box: Go / No Go
Average Rep Time:		Notes:		

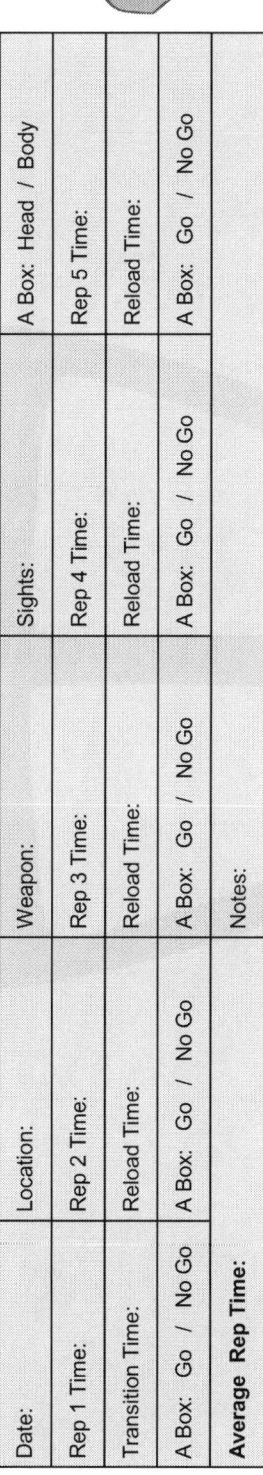

Date:	Location:	Weapon:	Sights:	A Box: Head / Body
Rep 1 Time:	Rep 2 Time:	Rep 3 Time:	Rep 4 Time:	Rep 5 Time:
Transition Time:	Reload Time:	Reload Time:	Reload Time:	Reload Time:
A Box: Go / No Go	A Box: Go / No Go	A Box: Go / No Go	A Box: Go / No Go	A Box: Go / No Go
Average Rep Time:		Notes:		

TRIGGER EFFECT

Purpose: Develop consistent accuracy and marksmanship follow through.

Distance: 10 Yards.

Target: 1.5 Inch square

Total Rounds Fired: 0 Rounds.

Repetitions: 10 Reps.

Starting Position & Condition: Start in the Standing - Carbine aimed at target. Condition 4 with hammer cocked.

Description: At your own personal go, aim at target and press trigger without moving the sights or red dot, keep the trigger pressed back for 5 seconds while keeping your aim on the target after you have pressed the trigger to break a dry fire shot. Rack the charging handle to reset the trigger and repeat 9 more times.

Goals: To be able to press the trigger, breaking the hammer, without moving the sight alignment or sight picture, and have consistent follow through.

1.5 Inch Square

www.GUNFIGHTERSERIES.com ©

TRIGGER EFFECT

Date:	Location:	Weapon:	Sights:	10 Reps?	Notes:
				Y / N	
				Y / N	
				Y / N	
				Y / N	
				Y / N	
				Y / N	
				Y / N	
				Y / N	
				Y / N	
				Y / N	
				Y / N	
				Y / N	
				Y / N	
				Y / N	
				Y / N	

Accuracy Drills - 1

TRIGGER EFFECT

www.GUNFIGHTERSERIES.com ©

Date:	Location:	Weapon:	Sights:	10 Reps?	Notes:
				Y / N	
				Y / N	
				Y / N	
				Y / N	
				Y / N	
				Y / N	
				Y / N	
				Y / N	
				Y / N	
				Y / N	
				Y / N	
				Y / N	
				Y / N	
				Y / N	
				Y / N	

TRIGGER EFFECT

Date:	Location:	Weapon:	Sights:	10 Reps?	Notes:
				Y / N	
				Y / N	
				Y / N	
				Y / N	
				Y / N	
				Y / N	
				Y / N	
				Y / N	
				Y / N	
				Y / N	
				Y / N	
				Y / N	
				Y / N	
				Y / N	
				Y / N	
				Y / N	

SOLID SHOT

Purpose: Develop consistent marksmanship follow through and trigger reset.

Distance: 10 Yards.

Target: 1.5 Inch square

Rounds Fired Per Rep: 1 Round.

Point Penalty: Go / No Go.

Repetitions: 10 Reps.

Total Rounds Fired: 10 Rounds.

Starting Position & Condition: Standing - Carbine aimed at target. Condition 1 with a magazine with 9 rounds in it.

Description: At your own personal go, aim at target, fire one round, while focusing on not moving the sights. Keep the trigger pressed back after the shot and keep your aim on the target after you have pressed the trigger to break the shot. While keeping your finger on the trigger, slowly release the trigger until you hear a click. Once you hear the click, do not let out anymore slack. Make sure of your aim and fire another shot, repeating the process until you have fired all of the repetitions.

Goals: To shoot all rounds within the square target. Any rounds outside or not touching the square is a No Go.

Variations: Add distance.

1.5 Inch Square

SOLID SHOT

Date:	Weapon:	Sling: Y / N	Notes:
Sights:	Positive Trigger Reset: Y / N	All 10 shots in: Y / N	

Date:	Weapon:	Sling: Y / N	Notes:
Sights:	Positive Trigger Reset: Y / N	All 10 shots in: Y / N	

Date:	Weapon:	Sling: Y / N	Notes:
Sights:	Positive Trigger Reset: Y / N	All 10 shots in: Y / N	

Date:	Weapon:	Sling: Y / N	Notes:
Sights:	Positive Trigger Reset: Y / N	All 10 shots in: Y / N	

Date:	Weapon:	Sling: Y / N	Notes:
Sights:	Positive Trigger Reset: Y / N	All 10 shots in: Y / N	

Fundamental Carbine ©

Accuracy Drills - 2

SOLID SHOT

Date:	Weapon:	Sling: Y / N	Notes:
Sights:	Positive Trigger Reset: Y / N	All 10 shots in: Y / N	

Date:	Weapon:	Sling: Y / N	Notes:
Sights:	Positive Trigger Reset: Y / N	All 10 shots in: Y / N	

Date:	Weapon:	Sling: Y / N	Notes:
Sights:	Positive Trigger Reset: Y / N	All 10 shots in: Y / N	

Date:	Weapon:	Sling: Y / N	Notes:
Sights:	Positive Trigger Reset: Y / N	All 10 shots in: Y / N	

Date:	Weapon:	Sling: Y / N	Notes:
Sights:	Positive Trigger Reset: Y / N	All 10 shots in: Y / N	

SOLID SHOT

Date:	Weapon:	Sling: Y / N	Notes:
Sights:	Positive Trigger Reset: Y / N	All 10 shots in: Y / N	

Date:	Weapon:	Sling: Y / N	Notes:
Sights:	Positive Trigger Reset: Y / N	All 10 shots in: Y / N	

Date:	Weapon:	Sling: Y / N	Notes:
Sights:	Positive Trigger Reset: Y / N	All 10 shots in: Y / N	

Date:	Weapon:	Sling: Y / N	Notes:
Sights:	Positive Trigger Reset: Y / N	All 10 shots in: Y / N	

Date:	Weapon:	Sling: Y / N	Notes:
Sights:	Positive Trigger Reset: Y / N	All 10 shots in: Y / N	

Accuracy Drills - 2

Fundamental Carbine ©

www.GUNFIGHTERSERIES.com ©

SOLID SHOT

Date:	Weapon:	Sling: Y / N	Notes:
Sights:	Positive Trigger Reset: Y / N	All 10 shots in: Y / N	

Date:	Weapon:	Sling: Y / N	Notes:
Sights:	Positive Trigger Reset: Y / N	All 10 shots in: Y / N	

Date:	Weapon:	Sling: Y / N	Notes:
Sights:	Positive Trigger Reset: Y / N	All 10 shots in: Y / N	

Date:	Weapon:	Sling: Y / N	Notes:
Sights:	Positive Trigger Reset: Y / N	All 10 shots in: Y / N	

Date:	Weapon:	Sling: Y / N	Notes:
Sights:	Positive Trigger Reset: Y / N	All 10 shots in: Y / N	

SOLID SHOT

Date:	Weapon:	Sling: Y / N	Notes:
Sights:	Positive Trigger Reset: Y / N	All 10 shots in: Y / N	

Date:	Weapon:	Sling: Y / N	Notes:
Sights:	Positive Trigger Reset: Y / N	All 10 shots in: Y / N	

Date:	Weapon:	Sling: Y / N	Notes:
Sights:	Positive Trigger Reset: Y / N	All 10 shots in: Y / N	

Date:	Weapon:	Sling: Y / N	Notes:
Sights:	Positive Trigger Reset: Y / N	All 10 shots in: Y / N	

Date:	Weapon:	Sling: Y / N	Notes:
Sights:	Positive Trigger Reset: Y / N	All 10 shots in: Y / N	

Accuracy Drills - 2

Fundamental Carbine ©

5 FOR 10

Purpose: Decrease shot anticipation and increase accuracy.

Distance: 10 Yards.

Target: 1.5 Inch squares X 5

Rounds Fired Per Rep: 5 Rounds.

Point Penalty: Go / No Go.

Repetitions: 5 Reps.

Total Rounds Fired: 25 Rounds.

Starting Position & Condition: Standing - Carbine aimed at target. Condition 1 with a magazine with 5 rounds in it.

Description: At a personal go, fire 5 rounds into the target. The goal is to get all rounds into the 1.5 inch square target. After you have fired 5 live rounds, unload the carbine and with the carbine in weapon condition 4 (No round in the chamber, no live rounds, no magazine but cocked), aim at the 1.5 inch square target and press the trigger dry firing without moving the sights for a repetition of 5 good dry fires. After you have dry fired 5 times, load the carbine with 5 more rounds and repeat the cycle of 5 live fired rounds and 5 dry fires for a total of 5 cycles. Taking your time and getting good accurate hits in the 1.5 inch target is the goal. The dry fires after the live fire may show that you are anticipating the shot if your carbine dips when you press the trigger, causing you to be less accurate than you could be.

Goals: To be able to press the trigger, breaking the hammer without moving the sight alignment or sight picture. Any rounds outside or not touching the square is a No Go.

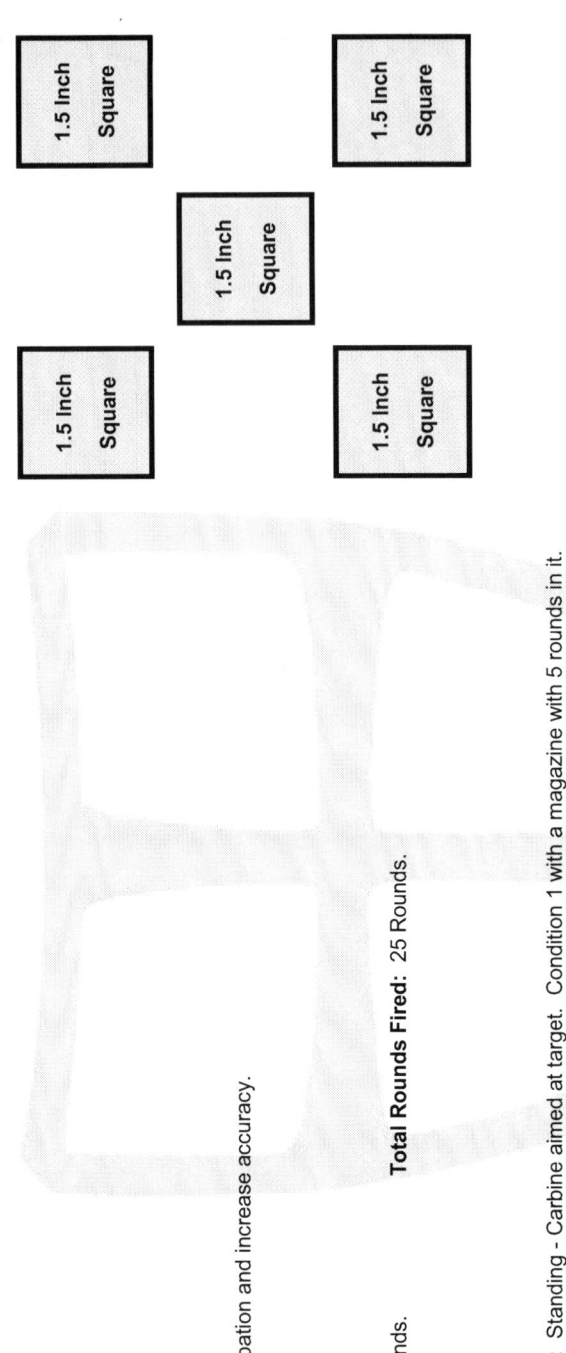

5 FOR 10

Date:	Weapon:	Sights:	Notes:
1st group all in: Y / N	2nd group all in: Y / N	3rd group all in: Y / N	4th group all in: Y / N	5th group all in: Y / N

Date:	Weapon:	Sights:	Notes:
1st group all in: Y / N	2nd group all in: Y / N	3rd group all in: Y / N	4th group all in: Y / N	5th group all in: Y / N

Date:	Weapon:	Sights:	Notes:
1st group all in: Y / N	2nd group all in: Y / N	3rd group all in: Y / N	4th group all in: Y / N	5th group all in: Y / N

Date:	Weapon:	Sights:	Notes:
1st group all in: Y / N	2nd group all in: Y / N	3rd group all in: Y / N	4th group all in: Y / N	5th group all in: Y / N

Date:	Weapon:	Sights:	Notes:
1st group all in: Y / N	2nd group all in: Y / N	3rd group all in: Y / N	4th group all in: Y / N	5th group all in: Y / N

Fundamental Carbine ©

Accuracy Drills - 3

5 FOR 10

www.GUNFIGHTERSERIES.com ©

Date:	Weapon:	Sights:	Notes:
1st group all in: Y / N	2nd group all in: Y / N	3rd group all in: Y / N	4th group all in: Y / N	5th group all in: Y / N

Date:	Weapon:	Sights:	Notes:
1st group all in: Y / N	2nd group all in: Y / N	3rd group all in: Y / N	4th group all in: Y / N	5th group all in: Y / N

Date:	Weapon:	Sights:	Notes:
1st group all in: Y / N	2nd group all in: Y / N	3rd group all in: Y / N	4th group all in: Y / N	5th group all in: Y / N

Date:	Weapon:	Sights:	Notes:
1st group all in: Y / N	2nd group all in: Y / N	3rd group all in: Y / N	4th group all in: Y / N	5th group all in: Y / N

Date:	Weapon:	Sights:	Notes:
1st group all in: Y / N	2nd group all in: Y / N	3rd group all in: Y / N	4th group all in: Y / N	5th group all in: Y / N

5 FOR 10

Date:	Weapon:	Sights:	Notes:
1st group all in: Y / N	2nd group all in: Y / N	3rd group all in: Y / N	4th group all in: Y / N	5th group all in: Y / N

Date:	Weapon:	Sights:	Notes:
1st group all in: Y / N	2nd group all in: Y / N	3rd group all in: Y / N	4th group all in: Y / N	5th group all in: Y / N

Date:	Weapon:	Sights:	Notes:
1st group all in: Y / N	2nd group all in: Y / N	3rd group all in: Y / N	4th group all in: Y / N	5th group all in: Y / N

Date:	Weapon:	Sights:	Notes:
1st group all in: Y / N	2nd group all in: Y / N	3rd group all in: Y / N	4th group all in: Y / N	5th group all in: Y / N

Date:	Weapon:	Sights:	Notes:
1st group all in: Y / N	2nd group all in: Y / N	3rd group all in: Y / N	4th group all in: Y / N	5th group all in: Y / N

5 FOR 10

www.GUNFIGHTERSERIES.com ©

Date:	Weapon:	Sights:	Notes:
1st group all in: Y / N	2nd group all in: Y / N	3rd group all in: Y / N	4th group all in: Y / N	5th group all in: Y / N

Date:	Weapon:	Sights:	Notes:
1st group all in: Y / N	2nd group all in: Y / N	3rd group all in: Y / N	4th group all in: Y / N	5th group all in: Y / N

Date:	Weapon:	Sights:	Notes:
1st group all in: Y / N	2nd group all in: Y / N	3rd group all in: Y / N	4th group all in: Y / N	5th group all in: Y / N

Date:	Weapon:	Sights:	Notes:
1st group all in: Y / N	2nd group all in: Y / N	3rd group all in: Y / N	4th group all in: Y / N	5th group all in: Y / N

Date:	Weapon:	Sights:	Notes:
1st group all in: Y / N	2nd group all in: Y / N	3rd group all in: Y / N	4th group all in: Y / N	5th group all in: Y / N

5 FOR 10

Date:	Weapon:	Sights:	Notes:	
1st group all in: Y / N	2nd group all in: Y / N	3rd group all in: Y / N	4th group all in: Y / N	5th group all in: Y / N

Date:	Weapon:	Sights:	Notes:	
1st group all in: Y / N	2nd group all in: Y / N	3rd group all in: Y / N	4th group all in: Y / N	5th group all in: Y / N

Date:	Weapon:	Sights:	Notes:	
1st group all in: Y / N	2nd group all in: Y / N	3rd group all in: Y / N	4th group all in: Y / N	5th group all in: Y / N

Date:	Weapon:	Sights:	Notes:	
1st group all in: Y / N	2nd group all in: Y / N	3rd group all in: Y / N	4th group all in: Y / N	5th group all in: Y / N

Date:	Weapon:	Sights:	Notes:	
1st group all in: Y / N	2nd group all in: Y / N	3rd group all in: Y / N	4th group all in: Y / N	5th group all in: Y / N

PIN POINT

Purpose: Accuracy with short distance hold over.

Distance: 5, 7, 10, 15, and 25 yards.

Target: GF-2

Rounds Fired Per Distance: 3 Rounds. **Total Rounds Fired:** 15 Rounds.

Point Penalty: As per target score.

Repetitions: 1 Rep.

Starting Position & Condition: Standing – Any carbine ready position you choose. Condition 1.

Description: At your own personal go, raise your carbine, take good aim and fire 3 rounds into the target from each distance of 5, 7, 10, 15 and 25 yards. The actual goal is to keep all rounds in the black. A Gunfighter score is going to be hard to do, but it can be done, so keep working at it. Take your time and make every shot count. There is no time limit and if you feel you are going to break a bad shot, stop and start that shot over.

Goals: Novice: Minimum of 135 points with all rounds in black. Expert: 150 Points. Gunfighter: 150 Points with 10 X's.

PIN POINT

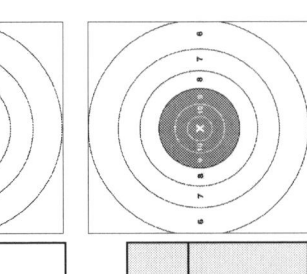

Date:	Location:	Weapon:	Sights
# of 6's:	# of 7's:	# of 8's:	Notes:
# of 9's:	# of 10's:	TOTAL SCORE: X's	

Date:	Location:	Weapon:	Sights
# of 6's:	# of 7's:	# of 8's:	Notes:
# of 9's:	# of 10's:	TOTAL SCORE: X's	

Date:	Location:	Weapon:	Sights
# of 6's:	# of 7's:	# of 8's:	Notes:
# of 9's:	# of 10's:	TOTAL SCORE: X's	

Date:	Location:	Weapon:	Sights
# of 6's:	# of 7's:	# of 8's:	Notes:
# of 9's:	# of 10's:	TOTAL SCORE: X's	

PIN POINT

www.GUNFIGHTERSERIES.com ©

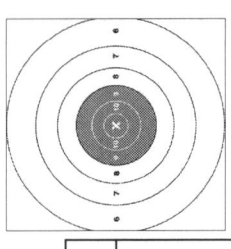
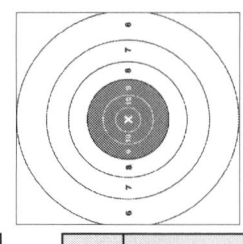
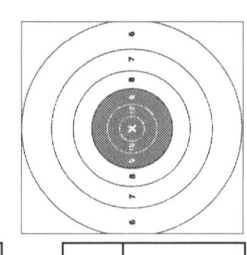
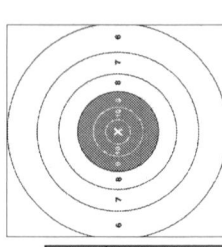

Date:	Location:	Weapon:	Sights
# of 6's:	# of 7's:	# of 8's:	Notes:
# of 9's:	# of 10's:	TOTAL SCORE: X's	

Date:	Location:	Weapon:	Sights
# of 6's:	# of 7's:	# of 8's:	Notes:
# of 9's:	# of 10's:	TOTAL SCORE: X's	

Date:	Location:	Weapon:	Sights
# of 6's:	# of 7's:	# of 8's:	Notes:
# of 9's:	# of 10's:	TOTAL SCORE: X's	

Date:	Location:	Weapon:	Sights
# of 6's:	# of 7's:	# of 8's:	Notes:
# of 9's:	# of 10's:	TOTAL SCORE: X's	

PIN POINT

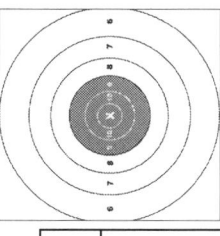
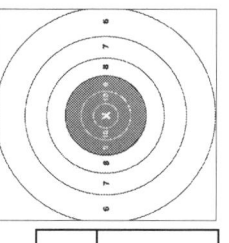
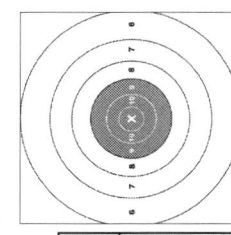

Target 1

Date:	Location:	Weapon:	Sights
# of 6's:	# of 7's:	# of 8's:	Notes:
# of 9's:	# of 10's:	TOTAL SCORE:	X's

Target 2

Date:	Location:	Weapon:	Sights
# of 6's:	# of 7's:	# of 8's:	Notes:
# of 9's:	# of 10's:	TOTAL SCORE:	X's

Target 3

Date:	Location:	Weapon:	Sights
# of 6's:	# of 7's:	# of 8's:	Notes:
# of 9's:	# of 10's:	TOTAL SCORE:	X's

Target 4

Date:	Location:	Weapon:	Sights
# of 6's:	# of 7's:	# of 8's:	Notes:
# of 9's:	# of 10's:	TOTAL SCORE:	X's

Accuracy Drills - 4

Fundamental Carbine ©

PIN POINT

www.GUNFIGHTERSERIES.com ©

Date:	Location:	Weapon:	Sights
# of 6's:	# of 7's:	# of 8's:	Notes:
# of 9's:	# of 10's:	TOTAL SCORE: X's	

Date:	Location:	Weapon:	Sights
# of 6's:	# of 7's:	# of 8's:	Notes:
# of 9's:	# of 10's:	TOTAL SCORE: X's	

Date:	Location:	Weapon:	Sights
# of 6's:	# of 7's:	# of 8's:	Notes:
# of 9's:	# of 10's:	TOTAL SCORE: X's	

Date:	Location:	Weapon:	Sights
# of 6's:	# of 7's:	# of 8's:	Notes:
# of 9's:	# of 10's:	TOTAL SCORE: X's	

PIN POINT

Date:	Location:	Weapon:	Sights
# of 6's:	# of 7's:	# of 8's:	Notes:
# of 9's:	# of 10's:	**TOTAL SCORE:** X's	

Date:	Location:	Weapon:	Sights
# of 6's:	# of 7's:	# of 8's:	Notes:
# of 9's:	# of 10's:	**TOTAL SCORE:** X's	

Date:	Location:	Weapon:	Sights
# of 6's:	# of 7's:	# of 8's:	Notes:
# of 9's:	# of 10's:	**TOTAL SCORE:** X's	

Date:	Location:	Weapon:	Sights
# of 6's:	# of 7's:	# of 8's:	Notes:
# of 9's:	# of 10's:	**TOTAL SCORE:** X's	

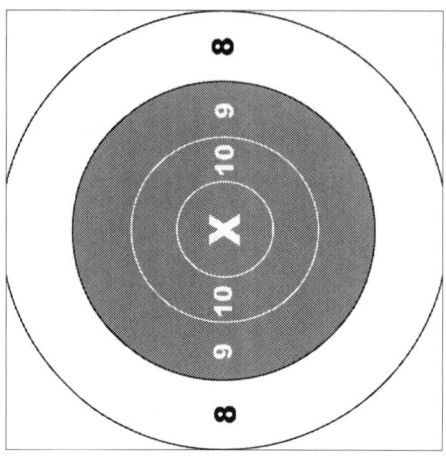

ROCK SOLID

Purpose: Accuracy with long distance hold over.

Distance: 10, 15, 25, 35, and 50 yards.

Target: GF-1

Rounds Fired Per Distance: 3 Rounds.

Total Rounds Fired: 15 Rounds.

Point Penalty: As per target score.

Repetitions: 1 Rep.

Starting Position & Condition: Standing – Any carbine ready position you choose. Condition 1.

Description: At your own personal go, raise your carbine, take good aim and fire 3 rounds into the target from each distance of 10, 15, 25, 35 and 50 yards. The actual goal is to keep all rounds in the black. Take your time and make every shot count. There is no time limit and if you feel you are going to break a bad shot, stop and start that shot over.

Goals: Novice: Minimum of 135 points with all rounds in black.   Expert: 150 Points.   Gunfighter: 150 Points with 10 X's.

Variation: Time the drill from start to finish.

ROCK SOLID

Date:	Location:	Weapon:	Sights
# of 8's:	# of 9's:	# of 10's:	Notes:
Drill Time:	TOTAL SCORE:	# of X's	

Date:	Location:	Weapon:	Sights
# of 8's:	# of 9's:	# of 10's:	Notes:
Drill Time:	TOTAL SCORE:	# of X's	

Date:	Location:	Weapon:	Sights
# of 8's:	# of 9's:	# of 10's:	Notes:
Drill Time:	TOTAL SCORE:	# of X's	

Date:	Location:	Weapon:	Sights
# of 8's:	# of 9's:	# of 10's:	Notes:
Drill Time:	TOTAL SCORE:	# of X's	

ROCK SOLID

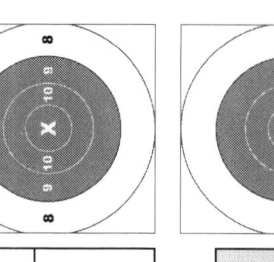 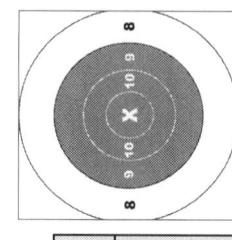 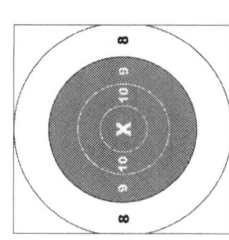 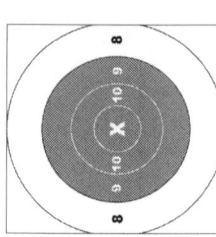

Date:	Location:	Weapon:	Sights
# of 8's:	# of 9's:	# of 10's:	Notes:
Drill Time:	TOTAL SCORE:	# of X's	

Date:	Location:	Weapon:	Sights
# of 8's:	# of 9's:	# of 10's:	Notes:
Drill Time:	TOTAL SCORE:	# of X's	

Date:	Location:	Weapon:	Sights
# of 8's:	# of 9's:	# of 10's:	Notes:
Drill Time:	TOTAL SCORE:	# of X's	

Date:	Location:	Weapon:	Sights
# of 8's:	# of 9's:	# of 10's:	Notes:
Drill Time:	TOTAL SCORE:	# of X's	

ROCK SOLID

Date:	Location:	Weapon:	Sights
# of 8's:	# of 9's:	# of 10's:	Notes:
Drill Time:	**TOTAL SCORE:**	**# of X's**	

Date:	Location:	Weapon:	Sights
# of 8's:	# of 9's:	# of 10's:	Notes:
Drill Time:	**TOTAL SCORE:**	**# of X's**	

Date:	Location:	Weapon:	Sights
# of 8's:	# of 9's:	# of 10's:	Notes:
Drill Time:	**TOTAL SCORE:**	**# of X's**	

Date:	Location:	Weapon:	Sights
# of 8's:	# of 9's:	# of 10's:	Notes:
Drill Time:	**TOTAL SCORE:**	**# of X's**	

ROCK SOLID

Date:	Location:	Weapon:	Sights
# of 8's:	# of 9's:	# of 10's:	Notes:
Drill Time:	TOTAL SCORE:	# of X's	

Date:	Location:	Weapon:	Sights
# of 8's:	# of 9's:	# of 10's:	Notes:
Drill Time:	TOTAL SCORE:	# of X's	

Date:	Location:	Weapon:	Sights
# of 8's:	# of 9's:	# of 10's:	Notes:
Drill Time:	TOTAL SCORE:	# of X's	

Date:	Location:	Weapon:	Sights
# of 8's:	# of 9's:	# of 10's:	Notes:
Drill Time:	TOTAL SCORE:	# of X's	

www.GUNFIGHTERSERIES.com ©

ROCK SOLID

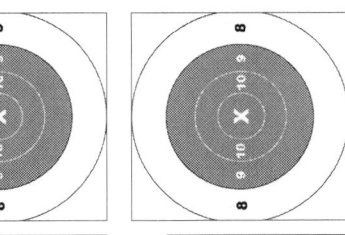

Date:	Location:	Weapon:	Sights
# of 8's:	# of 9's:	# of 10's:	Notes:
Drill Time:	TOTAL SCORE:	# of X's	

Date:	Location:	Weapon:	Sights
# of 8's:	# of 9's:	# of 10's:	Notes:
Drill Time:	TOTAL SCORE:	# of X's	

Date:	Location:	Weapon:	Sights
# of 8's:	# of 9's:	# of 10's:	Notes:
Drill Time:	TOTAL SCORE:	# of X's	

Date:	Location:	Weapon:	Sights
# of 8's:	# of 9's:	# of 10's:	Notes:
Drill Time:	TOTAL SCORE:	# of X's	

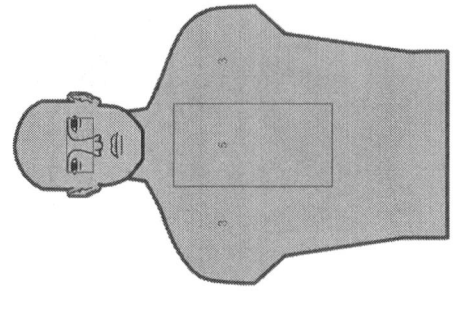

CARBINE LOW READY

Purpose: Increase competency of the use of the low ready position.

Distance: 10 Yards.

Target: JD-QUAL1

Par Time: 1 Second.

Extra Equipment Needed: Shot timer.

Total Rounds Fired: 5 Rounds.

Rounds Fired Per Rep: 1 Round.

Point Penalty: Go / No Go.

Repetitions: 5 Reps.

Starting Position & Condition: Standing - Low ready. Condition 1.

Description: Low ready position is the butt stock is on your shoulder with the muzzle pointed into the dirt 6 to 8 feet in front of you while you are looking at the target. From the low ready position, at the timer beep, raise the carbine and take aim at the target with a flash sight picture and fire a round within 1 second into the A Zone (5 point) body box. Record how many times you made par time and hit within the body box.

Variations: Shoot the head box, add distance, decrease time, or add .3 seconds for each additional shot you take.

www.GUNFIGHTERSERIES.com ©

CARBINE LOW READY

Date:	Location:	Weapon:	Sights:	Notes:
A Zone: Body / Head	# Under Par:	# In A Box:	Go / No Go	

Date:	Location:	Weapon:	Sights:	Notes:
A Zone: Body / Head	# Under Par:	# In A Box:	Go / No Go	

Date:	Location:	Weapon:	Sights:	Notes:
A Zone: Body / Head	# Under Par:	# In A Box:	Go / No Go	

Date:	Location:	Weapon:	Sights:	Notes:
A Zone: Body / Head	# Under Par:	# In A Box:	Go / No Go	

Date:	Location:	Weapon:	Sights:	Notes:
A Zone: Body / Head	# Under Par:	# In A Box:	Go / No Go	

Ready Position Drills - 1

Fundamental Carbine ©

CARBINE LOW READY

Date:	Location:	Weapon:	Sights:	Notes:
A Zone: Body / Head	# Under Par:	# In A Box:	Go / No Go	

Date:	Location:	Weapon:	Sights:	Notes:
A Zone: Body / Head	# Under Par:	# In A Box:	Go / No Go	

Date:	Location:	Weapon:	Sights:	Notes:
A Zone: Body / Head	# Under Par:	# In A Box:	Go / No Go	

Date:	Location:	Weapon:	Sights:	Notes:
A Zone: Body / Head	# Under Par:	# In A Box:	Go / No Go	

Date:	Location:	Weapon:	Sights:	Notes:
A Zone: Body / Head	# Under Par:	# In A Box:	Go / No Go	

www.GUNFIGHTERSERIES.com ©

CARBINE LOW READY

Date:	Location:	Weapon:	Sights:	Notes:
A Zone: Body / Head	# Under Par:	# In A Box:	**Go / No Go**	

Date:	Location:	Weapon:	Sights:	Notes:
A Zone: Body / Head	# Under Par:	# In A Box:	**Go / No Go**	

Date:	Location:	Weapon:	Sights:	Notes:
A Zone: Body / Head	# Under Par:	# In A Box:	**Go / No Go**	

Date:	Location:	Weapon:	Sights:	Notes:
A Zone: Body / Head	# Under Par:	# In A Box:	**Go / No Go**	

Date:	Location:	Weapon:	Sights:	Notes:
A Zone: Body / Head	# Under Par:	# In A Box:	**Go / No Go**	

Ready Position Drills - 1

Fundamental Carbine ©

CARBINE LOW READY

www.GUNFIGHTERSERIES.com ©

Date:	Location:	Weapon:	Sights:	Notes:
A Zone: Body / Head	# Under Par:	# In A Box:	Go / No Go	

Date:	Location:	Weapon:	Sights:	Notes:
A Zone: Body / Head	# Under Par:	# In A Box:	Go / No Go	

Date:	Location:	Weapon:	Sights:	Notes:
A Zone: Body / Head	# Under Par:	# In A Box:	Go / No Go	

Date:	Location:	Weapon:	Sights:	Notes:
A Zone: Body / Head	# Under Par:	# In A Box:	Go / No Go	

Date:	Location:	Weapon:	Sights:	Notes:
A Zone: Body / Head	# Under Par:	# In A Box:	Go / No Go	

CARBINE LOW READY

Date:	Location:	Weapon:	Sights:	Notes:
A Zone: Body / Head	# Under Par:	# In A Box:	Go / No Go	

Date:	Location:	Weapon:	Sights:	Notes:
A Zone: Body / Head	# Under Par:	# In A Box:	Go / No Go	

Date:	Location:	Weapon:	Sights:	Notes:
A Zone: Body / Head	# Under Par:	# In A Box:	Go / No Go	

Date:	Location:	Weapon:	Sights:	Notes:
A Zone: Body / Head	# Under Par:	# In A Box:	Go / No Go	

Date:	Location:	Weapon:	Sights:	Notes:
A Zone: Body / Head	# Under Par:	# In A Box:	Go / No Go	

Ready Position Drills - 1

Fundamental Carbine ©

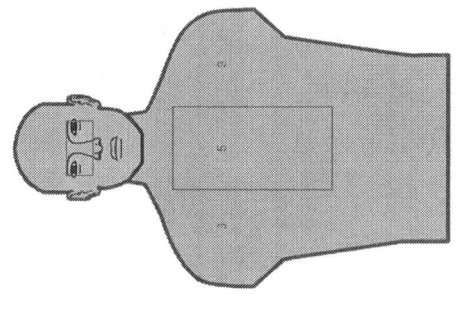

CARBINE READY

Purpose: Increase competency of the use of the ready position.

Distance: 10 Yards.

Target: JD-QUAL1

Par Time: 0.8 Seconds.

Extra Equipment Needed: Shot timer.

Rounds Fired Per Rep: 1 Round.

Total Rounds Fired: 5 Rounds.

Point Penalty: Go / No Go.

Repetitions: 5 Reps.

Starting Position & Condition: Standing - Ready. Condition 1.

Description: The ready position is the butt stock on your shoulder with the muzzle pointed in the direction of the target while you are looking at the target just over the top of the sights. From the ready position, at the timer beep, raise the carbine and take aim at the target with a flash sight picture and fire a round within .8 seconds into the A Zone (5 point) body box. Record how many times you made par time and hit within the A Zone (5 point) body box.

Variations: Shoot the head box, add distance, decrease time, or add .3 seconds for each additional shot you take.

CARBINE READY

Date:	Location:	Weapon:	Sights:	Notes:
A Zone: Body / Head	# Under Par:	# In A Box:	Go / No Go	

Date:	Location:	Weapon:	Sights:	Notes:
A Zone: Body / Head	# Under Par:	# In A Box:	Go / No Go	

Date:	Location:	Weapon:	Sights:	Notes:
A Zone: Body / Head	# Under Par:	# In A Box:	Go / No Go	

Date:	Location:	Weapon:	Sights:	Notes:
A Zone: Body / Head	# Under Par:	# In A Box:	Go / No Go	

Date:	Location:	Weapon:	Sights:	Notes:
A Zone: Body / Head	# Under Par:	# In A Box:	Go / No Go	

Ready Position Drills - 2

Fundamental Carbine ©

CARBINE READY

www.GUNFIGHTERSERIES.com ©

Date:	Location:	Weapon:	Sights:	Notes:
A Zone: Body / Head	# Under Par:	# In A Box:	Go / No Go	

Date:	Location:	Weapon:	Sights:	Notes:
A Zone: Body / Head	# Under Par:	# In A Box:	Go / No Go	

Date:	Location:	Weapon:	Sights:	Notes:
A Zone: Body / Head	# Under Par:	# In A Box:	Go / No Go	

Date:	Location:	Weapon:	Sights:	Notes:
A Zone: Body / Head	# Under Par:	# In A Box:	Go / No Go	

Date:	Location:	Weapon:	Sights:	Notes:
A Zone: Body / Head	# Under Par:	# In A Box:	Go / No Go	

CARBINE READY

Date:	Location:	Weapon:	Sights:	Notes:
A Zone: Body / Head	# Under Par:	# In A Box:	Go / No Go	

Date:	Location:	Weapon:	Sights:	Notes:
A Zone: Body / Head	# Under Par:	# In A Box:	Go / No Go	

Date:	Location:	Weapon:	Sights:	Notes:
A Zone: Body / Head	# Under Par:	# In A Box:	Go / No Go	

Date:	Location:	Weapon:	Sights:	Notes:
A Zone: Body / Head	# Under Par:	# In A Box:	Go / No Go	

Date:	Location:	Weapon:	Sights:	Notes:
A Zone: Body / Head	# Under Par:	# In A Box:	Go / No Go	

Ready Position Drills - 2

Fundamental Carbine ©

CARBINE READY

Date:	Location:	Weapon:	Sights:	Notes:
A Zone: Body / Head	# Under Par:	# In A Box:	Go / No Go	

Date:	Location:	Weapon:	Sights:	Notes:
A Zone: Body / Head	# Under Par:	# In A Box:	Go / No Go	

Date:	Location:	Weapon:	Sights:	Notes:
A Zone: Body / Head	# Under Par:	# In A Box:	Go / No Go	

Date:	Location:	Weapon:	Sights:	Notes:
A Zone: Body / Head	# Under Par:	# In A Box:	Go / No Go	

Date:	Location:	Weapon:	Sights:	Notes:
A Zone: Body / Head	# Under Par:	# In A Box:	Go / No Go	

www.GUNFIGHTERSERIES.com ©

CARBINE READY

Date:	Location:	Weapon:	Sights:	Notes:
A Zone: Body / Head	# Under Par:	# In A Box:	**Go / No Go**	

Date:	Location:	Weapon:	Sights:	Notes:
A Zone: Body / Head	# Under Par:	# In A Box:	**Go / No Go**	

Date:	Location:	Weapon:	Sights:	Notes:
A Zone: Body / Head	# Under Par:	# In A Box:	**Go / No Go**	

Date:	Location:	Weapon:	Sights:	Notes:
A Zone: Body / Head	# Under Par:	# In A Box:	**Go / No Go**	

Date:	Location:	Weapon:	Sights:	Notes:
A Zone: Body / Head	# Under Par:	# In A Box:	**Go / No Go**	

Ready Position Drills - 2

Fundamental Carbine ©

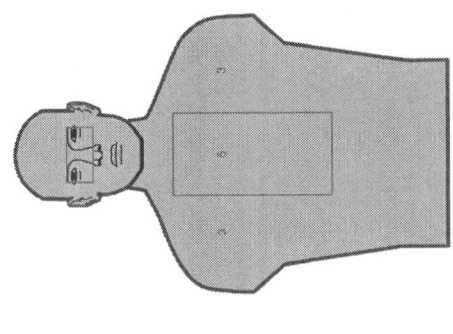

CARBINE HIGH READY

Purpose: Increase competency of the use of the high ready position.

Distance: 10 Yards.

Target: JD-QUAL1

Par Time: 1.2 Seconds.

Extra Equipment Needed: Shot timer.

Rounds Fired Per Rep: 1 Round.

Total Rounds Fired: 5 Rounds.

Point Penalty: Go / No Go.

Repetitions: 5 Reps.

Starting Position & Condition: Standing - High ready. Condition 1.

Description: The high ready position is where the butt stock is at the side of your hip with the muzzle pointed in the upward at a roughly 60 degree angle at the direction of the target while you are looking at the target just over parallel to the top of the front sight. From the high ready position, at the timer beep, raise the carbine and take aim at the target with a flash sight picture and fire a round within 1.2 seconds into the A Zone (5 point) body box. Record how many times you made par time and hit within the A Zone (5 point) body box.

Variations: Shoot the head box, add distance, decrease time, or add .3 seconds for each additional shot you take.

CARBINE HIGH READY

Date:	Location:	Weapon:	Sights:	Notes:
A Zone: Body / Head	# Under Par:	# In A Box:	**Go / No Go**	

Date:	Location:	Weapon:	Sights:	Notes:
A Zone: Body / Head	# Under Par:	# In A Box:	**Go / No Go**	

Date:	Location:	Weapon:	Sights:	Notes:
A Zone: Body / Head	# Under Par:	# In A Box:	**Go / No Go**	

Date:	Location:	Weapon:	Sights:	Notes:
A Zone: Body / Head	# Under Par:	# In A Box:	**Go / No Go**	

Date:	Location:	Weapon:	Sights:	Notes:
A Zone: Body / Head	# Under Par:	# In A Box:	**Go / No Go**	

Ready Position Drills - 3

Fundamental Carbine ©

CARBINE HIGH READY

www.GUNFIGHTERSERIES.com ©

Date:	Location:	Weapon:	Sights:	Notes:
A Zone: Body / Head	# Under Par:	# In A Box:	**Go / No Go**	

Date:	Location:	Weapon:	Sights:	Notes:
A Zone: Body / Head	# Under Par:	# In A Box:	**Go / No Go**	

Date:	Location:	Weapon:	Sights:	Notes:
A Zone: Body / Head	# Under Par:	# In A Box:	**Go / No Go**	

Date:	Location:	Weapon:	Sights:	Notes:
A Zone: Body / Head	# Under Par:	# In A Box:	**Go / No Go**	

Date:	Location:	Weapon:	Sights:	Notes:
A Zone: Body / Head	# Under Par:	# In A Box:	**Go / No Go**	

CARBINE HIGH READY

Date:	Location:	Weapon:	Sights:	Notes:
A Zone: Body / Head	# Under Par:	# In A Box:	**Go / No Go**	

Date:	Location:	Weapon:	Sights:	Notes:
A Zone: Body / Head	# Under Par:	# In A Box:	**Go / No Go**	

Date:	Location:	Weapon:	Sights:	Notes:
A Zone: Body / Head	# Under Par:	# In A Box:	**Go / No Go**	

Date:	Location:	Weapon:	Sights:	Notes:
A Zone: Body / Head	# Under Par:	# In A Box:	**Go / No Go**	

Date:	Location:	Weapon:	Sights:	Notes:
A Zone: Body / Head	# Under Par:	# In A Box:	**Go / No Go**	

Ready Position Drills - 3

Fundamental Carbine ©

CARBINE HIGH READY

Date:	Location:	Weapon:	Sights:	Notes:
A Zone: Body / Head	# Under Par:	# In A Box:	Go / No Go	

Date:	Location:	Weapon:	Sights:	Notes:
A Zone: Body / Head	# Under Par:	# In A Box:	Go / No Go	

Date:	Location:	Weapon:	Sights:	Notes:
A Zone: Body / Head	# Under Par:	# In A Box:	Go / No Go	

Date:	Location:	Weapon:	Sights:	Notes:
A Zone: Body / Head	# Under Par:	# In A Box:	Go / No Go	

Date:	Location:	Weapon:	Sights:	Notes:
A Zone: Body / Head	# Under Par:	# In A Box:	Go / No Go	

www.GUNFIGHTERSERIES.com ©

CARBINE HIGH READY

Date:	Location:	Weapon:	Sights:	Notes:
A Zone: Body / Head	# Under Par:	# In A Box:	Go / No Go	

Date:	Location:	Weapon:	Sights:	Notes:
A Zone: Body / Head	# Under Par:	# In A Box:	Go / No Go	

Date:	Location:	Weapon:	Sights:	Notes:
A Zone: Body / Head	# Under Par:	# In A Box:	Go / No Go	

Date:	Location:	Weapon:	Sights:	Notes:
A Zone: Body / Head	# Under Par:	# In A Box:	Go / No Go	

Date:	Location:	Weapon:	Sights:	Notes:
A Zone: Body / Head	# Under Par:	# In A Box:	Go / No Go	

Ready Position Drills - 3

Fundamental Carbine ©

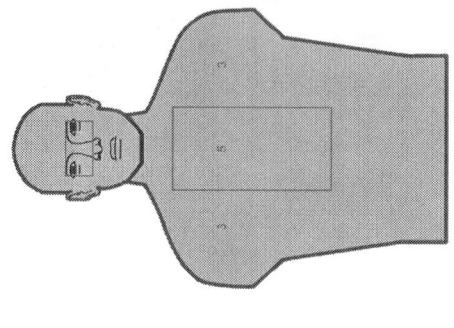

CARBINE PORT READY

Purpose: Increase competency of the use of the port ready position.

Distance: 10 Yards.

Target: JD-QUAL1

Par Time: 1.5 Seconds.

Extra Equipment Needed: Shot timer.

Rounds Fired Per Rep: 1 Round.   **Total Rounds Fired:** 5 Rounds.

Point Penalty: Go / No Go.

Repetitions: 5 Reps.

Starting Position & Condition: Standing - Port ready. Condition 1.

Description: The port ready position is where the butt stock is tucked into your side with the muzzle pointed straight upward while your non-firing hand does or does not hold onto the forearm of the carbine. From the port ready position, at the beep of the timer, mount the carbine and take aim at the target with a flash sight picture and fire a round within 1.5 seconds into the A Zone (5 point) body box. Record how many times you made par time and hit within the A Zone (5 point) body box.

Variations: Shoot the head box, add distance, decrease time, or add .3 seconds for each additional shot you take.

CARBINE PORT READY

Date:	Location:	Weapon:	Sights:	Notes:
A Zone: Body / Head	# Under Par:	# In A Box:	Go / No Go	

Date:	Location:	Weapon:	Sights:	Notes:
A Zone: Body / Head	# Under Par:	# In A Box:	Go / No Go	

Date:	Location:	Weapon:	Sights:	Notes:
A Zone: Body / Head	# Under Par:	# In A Box:	Go / No Go	

Date:	Location:	Weapon:	Sights:	Notes:
A Zone: Body / Head	# Under Par:	# In A Box:	Go / No Go	

Date:	Location:	Weapon:	Sights:	Notes:
A Zone: Body / Head	# Under Par:	# In A Box:	Go / No Go	

Ready Position Drills - 4

Fundamental Carbine ©

CARBINE PORT READY

www.GUNFIGHTERSERIES.com ©

Date:	Location:	Weapon:	Sights:	Notes:
A Zone: Body / Head	# Under Par:	# In A Box:	Go / No Go	

Date:	Location:	Weapon:	Sights:	Notes:
A Zone: Body / Head	# Under Par:	# In A Box:	Go / No Go	

Date:	Location:	Weapon:	Sights:	Notes:
A Zone: Body / Head	# Under Par:	# In A Box:	Go / No Go	

Date:	Location:	Weapon:	Sights:	Notes:
A Zone: Body / Head	# Under Par:	# In A Box:	Go / No Go	

Date:	Location:	Weapon:	Sights:	Notes:
A Zone: Body / Head	# Under Par:	# In A Box:	Go / No Go	

CARBINE PORT READY

Date:	Location:	Weapon:	Sights:	Notes:
A Zone: Body / Head	# Under Par:	# In A Box:	Go / No Go	

Date:	Location:	Weapon:	Sights:	Notes:
A Zone: Body / Head	# Under Par:	# In A Box:	Go / No Go	

Date:	Location:	Weapon:	Sights:	Notes:
A Zone: Body / Head	# Under Par:	# In A Box:	Go / No Go	

Date:	Location:	Weapon:	Sights:	Notes:
A Zone: Body / Head	# Under Par:	# In A Box:	Go / No Go	

Date:	Location:	Weapon:	Sights:	Notes:
A Zone: Body / Head	# Under Par:	# In A Box:	Go / No Go	

Ready Position Drills - 4

Fundamental Carbine ©

CARBINE PORT READY

Date:	Location:	Weapon:	Sights:	Notes:
A Zone: Body / Head	# Under Par:	# In A Box:	Go / No Go	

Date:	Location:	Weapon:	Sights:	Notes:
A Zone: Body / Head	# Under Par:	# In A Box:	Go / No Go	

Date:	Location:	Weapon:	Sights:	Notes:
A Zone: Body / Head	# Under Par:	# In A Box:	Go / No Go	

Date:	Location:	Weapon:	Sights:	Notes:
A Zone: Body / Head	# Under Par:	# In A Box:	Go / No Go	

Date:	Location:	Weapon:	Sights:	Notes:
A Zone: Body / Head	# Under Par:	# In A Box:	Go / No Go	

www.GUNFIGHTERSERIES.com ©

CARBINE PORT READY

Date:	Location:	Weapon:	Sights:	Notes:
A Zone: Body / Head	# Under Par:	# In A Box:	Go / No Go	

Date:	Location:	Weapon:	Sights:	Notes:
A Zone: Body / Head	# Under Par:	# In A Box:	Go / No Go	

Date:	Location:	Weapon:	Sights:	Notes:
A Zone: Body / Head	# Under Par:	# In A Box:	Go / No Go	

Date:	Location:	Weapon:	Sights:	Notes:
A Zone: Body / Head	# Under Par:	# In A Box:	Go / No Go	

Date:	Location:	Weapon:	Sights:	Notes:
A Zone: Body / Head	# Under Par:	# In A Box:	Go / No Go	

Ready Position Drills - 4

Fundamental Carbine ©

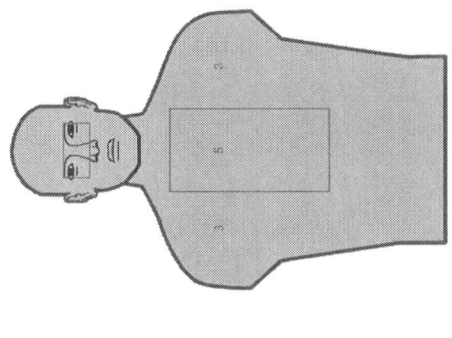

CARBINE TACTICAL READY

Purpose: Increase competency of the use of the tactical ready position.

Distance: 10 Yards.

Target: JD-QUAL1

Par Time: 1.2 Seconds.

Extra Equipment Needed: Shot timer.

Rounds Fired Per Rep: 1 Round.

Point Penalty: Go / No Go.

Repetitions: 5 Reps.

Total Rounds Fired: 5 Rounds.

Starting Position & Condition: Standing - Tactical ready. Condition 1.

Description: The tactical ready position is with the carbine turned on its side and the butt stock is placed in front of your shoulder with the muzzle pointed in the direction of the ground 6 to 8 inches in front of your feet. Your support hand will be supporting the forearm/handguard. From the tactical ready position, at the timer beep, raise the carbine and take aim at the target with a flash sight picture and fire a round within 1.2 seconds into the A Zone (5 point) body box. Record how many times you made par time and hit within the A Zone (5 point) body box.

Variations: Shoot the head box, add distance, decrease time, or add .3 seconds for each additional shot you take.

CARBINE TACTICAL READY

Date:	Location:	Weapon:	Sights:	Notes:
A Zone: Body / Head	# Under Par:	# In A Box:	**Go / No Go**	

Date:	Location:	Weapon:	Sights:	Notes:
A Zone: Body / Head	# Under Par:	# In A Box:	**Go / No Go**	

Date:	Location:	Weapon:	Sights:	Notes:
A Zone: Body / Head	# Under Par:	# In A Box:	**Go / No Go**	

Date:	Location:	Weapon:	Sights:	Notes:
A Zone: Body / Head	# Under Par:	# In A Box:	**Go / No Go**	

Date:	Location:	Weapon:	Sights:	Notes:
A Zone: Body / Head	# Under Par:	# In A Box:	**Go / No Go**	

Fundamental Carbine ©

Ready Position Drills - 5

CARBINE TACTICAL READY

Date:	Location:	Weapon:	Sights:	Notes:
A Zone: Body / Head	# Under Par:	# In A Box:	Go / No Go	

Date:	Location:	Weapon:	Sights:	Notes:
A Zone: Body / Head	# Under Par:	# In A Box:	Go / No Go	

Date:	Location:	Weapon:	Sights:	Notes:
A Zone: Body / Head	# Under Par:	# In A Box:	Go / No Go	

Date:	Location:	Weapon:	Sights:	Notes:
A Zone: Body / Head	# Under Par:	# In A Box:	Go / No Go	

Date:	Location:	Weapon:	Sights:	Notes:
A Zone: Body / Head	# Under Par:	# In A Box:	Go / No Go	

www.GUNFIGHTERSERIES.com ©

CARBINE TACTICAL READY

Date:	Location:	Weapon:	Sights:	Notes:
A Zone: Body / Head	# Under Par:	# In A Box:	Go / No Go	

Date:	Location:	Weapon:	Sights:	Notes:
A Zone: Body / Head	# Under Par:	# In A Box:	Go / No Go	

Date:	Location:	Weapon:	Sights:	Notes:
A Zone: Body / Head	# Under Par:	# In A Box:	Go / No Go	

Date:	Location:	Weapon:	Sights:	Notes:
A Zone: Body / Head	# Under Par:	# In A Box:	Go / No Go	

Date:	Location:	Weapon:	Sights:	Notes:
A Zone: Body / Head	# Under Par:	# In A Box:	Go / No Go	

Ready Position Drills - 5

Fundamental Carbine ©

CARBINE TACTICAL READY

www.GUNFIGHTERSERIES.com ©

Date:	Location:	Weapon:	Sights:	Notes:
A Zone: Body / Head	# Under Par:	# In A Box:	**Go / No Go**	

Date:	Location:	Weapon:	Sights:	Notes:
A Zone: Body / Head	# Under Par:	# In A Box:	**Go / No Go**	

Date:	Location:	Weapon:	Sights:	Notes:
A Zone: Body / Head	# Under Par:	# In A Box:	**Go / No Go**	

Date:	Location:	Weapon:	Sights:	Notes:
A Zone: Body / Head	# Under Par:	# In A Box:	**Go / No Go**	

Date:	Location:	Weapon:	Sights:	Notes:
A Zone: Body / Head	# Under Par:	# In A Box:	**Go / No Go**	

CARBINE TACTICAL READY

Date:	Location:	Weapon:	Sights:	Notes:
A Zone: Body / Head	# Under Par:	# In A Box:	**Go / No Go**	

Date:	Location:	Weapon:	Sights:	Notes:
A Zone: Body / Head	# Under Par:	# In A Box:	**Go / No Go**	

Date:	Location:	Weapon:	Sights:	Notes:
A Zone: Body / Head	# Under Par:	# In A Box:	**Go / No Go**	

Date:	Location:	Weapon:	Sights:	Notes:
A Zone: Body / Head	# Under Par:	# In A Box:	**Go / No Go**	

Date:	Location:	Weapon:	Sights:	Notes:
A Zone: Body / Head	# Under Par:	# In A Box:	**Go / No Go**	

Fundamental Carbine ©

Ready Position Drills - 5

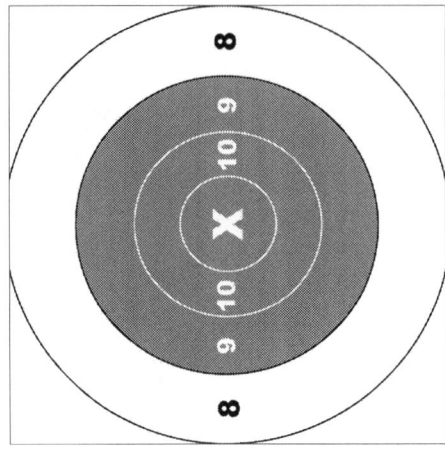

UNDER CONTROL

Purpose: Increase competency and accuracy of the use of quickly controlled fire.

Distance: 10 Yards.

Target: GF-1

Par Time: 2 Seconds.

Extra Equipment Needed: Shot timer.

Rounds Fired Per Rep: 2 Rounds.   **Total Rounds Fired:** 10 Rounds.

Point Penalty: As per target score.

Repetitions: 5 Reps.

Starting Position & Condition: Standing - Low Ready. Condition 1.

Description: At the timer beep, fire 2 rounds into the target within 2 seconds. The key to this drill is to shoot two quickly aimed shots within the time limit. Repeat drill 5 times. Score points for a total. If any of the repetitions failed to make the par time, the drill is a failure.

Goals: Novice: 90 Points within par.   Expert: 100 Points within par.   Gunfighter: 100 points - 10 X within par.

Variations: Advanced shooters can use a par time of 1.5 seconds.

www.GUNFIGHTERSERIES.com ©

UNDER CONTROL

Date:	Location:	Weapon:	Sights	Par: 2 Sec / 1.5 Sec	Notes:
Rep 1 Time:	Rep 2 Time:	Rep 3 Time:	Rep 4 Time:	Rep 5 Time:	
Reps Under Par:		Ave Time:	Total Score:	# of X's:	
Date:	Location:	Weapon:	Sights	Par: 2 Sec / 1.5 Sec	Notes:
Rep 1 Time:	Rep 2 Time:	Rep 3 Time:	Rep 4 Time:	Rep 5 Time:	
Reps Under Par:		Ave Time:	Total Score:	# of X's:	
Date:	Location:	Weapon:	Sights	Par: 2 Sec / 1.5 Sec	Notes:
Rep 1 Time:	Rep 2 Time:	Rep 3 Time:	Rep 4 Time:	Rep 5 Time:	
Reps Under Par:		Ave Time:	Total Score:	# of X's:	
Date:	Location:	Weapon:	Sights	Par: 2 Sec / 1.5 Sec	Notes:
Rep 1 Time:	Rep 2 Time:	Rep 3 Time:	Rep 4 Time:	Rep 5 Time:	
Reps Under Par:		Ave Time:	Total Score:	# of X's:	
Date:	Location:	Weapon:	Sights	Par: 2 Sec / 1.5 Sec	Notes:
Rep 1 Time:	Rep 2 Time:	Rep 3 Time:	Rep 4 Time:	Rep 5 Time:	
Reps Under Par:		Ave Time:	Total Score:	# of X's:	

UNDER CONTROL

Date:	Location:	Weapon:	Sights	Par: 2 Sec / 1.5 Sec	Notes:
Rep 1 Time:	Rep 2 Time:	Rep 3 Time:	Rep 4 Time:	Rep 5 Time:	
Reps Under Par:		Ave Time:	Total Score:	# of X's:	
Date:	Location:	Weapon:	Sights	Par: 2 Sec / 1.5 Sec	Notes:
Rep 1 Time:	Rep 2 Time:	Rep 3 Time:	Rep 4 Time:	Rep 5 Time:	
Reps Under Par:		Ave Time:	Total Score:	# of X's:	
Date:	Location:	Weapon:	Sights	Par: 2 Sec / 1.5 Sec	Notes:
Rep 1 Time:	Rep 2 Time:	Rep 3 Time:	Rep 4 Time:	Rep 5 Time:	
Reps Under Par:		Ave Time:	Total Score:	# of X's:	
Date:	Location:	Weapon:	Sights	Par: 2 Sec / 1.5 Sec	Notes:
Rep 1 Time:	Rep 2 Time:	Rep 3 Time:	Rep 4 Time:	Rep 5 Time:	
Reps Under Par:		Ave Time:	Total Score:	# of X's:	
Date:	Location:	Weapon:	Sights	Par: 2 Sec / 1.5 Sec	Notes:
Rep 1 Time:	Rep 2 Time:	Rep 3 Time:	Rep 4 Time:	Rep 5 Time:	
Reps Under Par:		Ave Time:	Total Score:	# of X's:	

UNDER CONTROL

Date:	Location:	Weapon:	Sights	Par: 2 Sec / 1.5 Sec	Notes:
Rep 1 Time:	Rep 2 Time:	Rep 3 Time:	Rep 4 Time:	Rep 5 Time:	
Reps Under Par:		Ave Time:	**Total Score:**	**# of X's:**	
Date:	Location:	Weapon:	Sights	Par: 2 Sec / 1.5 Sec	Notes:
Rep 1 Time:	Rep 2 Time:	Rep 3 Time:	Rep 4 Time:	Rep 5 Time:	
Reps Under Par:		Ave Time:	**Total Score:**	**# of X's:**	
Date:	Location:	Weapon:	Sights	Par: 2 Sec / 1.5 Sec	Notes:
Rep 1 Time:	Rep 2 Time:	Rep 3 Time:	Rep 4 Time:	Rep 5 Time:	
Reps Under Par:		Ave Time:	**Total Score:**	**# of X's:**	
Date:	Location:	Weapon:	Sights	Par: 2 Sec / 1.5 Sec	Notes:
Rep 1 Time:	Rep 2 Time:	Rep 3 Time:	Rep 4 Time:	Rep 5 Time:	
Reps Under Par:		Ave Time:	**Total Score:**	**# of X's:**	
Date:	Location:	Weapon:	Sights	Par: 2 Sec / 1.5 Sec	Notes:
Rep 1 Time:	Rep 2 Time:	Rep 3 Time:	Rep 4 Time:	Rep 5 Time:	
Reps Under Par:		Ave Time:	**Total Score:**	**# of X's:**	

Fundamental Carbine ©

Recoil Management - 1

UNDER CONTROL

Date:	Location:	Weapon:	Sights	Par: 2 Sec / 1.5 Sec	Notes:
Rep 1 Time:	Rep 2 Time:	Rep 3 Time:	Rep 4 Time:	Rep 5 Time:	
Reps Under Par:		Ave Time:	**Total Score:**	**# of X's:**	
Date:	Location:	Weapon:	Sights	Par: 2 Sec / 1.5 Sec	Notes:
Rep 1 Time:	Rep 2 Time:	Rep 3 Time:	Rep 4 Time:	Rep 5 Time:	
Reps Under Par:		Ave Time:	**Total Score:**	**# of X's:**	
Date:	Location:	Weapon:	Sights	Par: 2 Sec / 1.5 Sec	Notes:
Rep 1 Time:	Rep 2 Time:	Rep 3 Time:	Rep 4 Time:	Rep 5 Time:	
Reps Under Par:		Ave Time:	**Total Score:**	**# of X's:**	
Date:	Location:	Weapon:	Sights	Par: 2 Sec / 1.5 Sec	Notes:
Rep 1 Time:	Rep 2 Time:	Rep 3 Time:	Rep 4 Time:	Rep 5 Time:	
Reps Under Par:		Ave Time:	**Total Score:**	**# of X's:**	
Date:	Location:	Weapon:	Sights	Par: 2 Sec / 1.5 Sec	Notes:
Rep 1 Time:	Rep 2 Time:	Rep 3 Time:	Rep 4 Time:	Rep 5 Time:	
Reps Under Par:		Ave Time:	**Total Score:**	**# of X's:**	

UNDER CONTROL

Date:	Location:	Weapon:	Sights	Par: 2 Sec / 1.5 Sec	Notes:
Rep 1 Time:	Rep 2 Time:	Rep 3 Time:	Rep 4 Time:	Rep 5 Time:	
Reps Under Par:		Ave Time:	Total Score:	# of X's:	
Date:	Location:	Weapon:	Sights	Par: 2 Sec / 1.5 Sec	Notes:
Rep 1 Time:	Rep 2 Time:	Rep 3 Time:	Rep 4 Time:	Rep 5 Time:	
Reps Under Par:		Ave Time:	Total Score:	# of X's:	
Date:	Location:	Weapon:	Sights	Par: 2 Sec / 1.5 Sec	Notes:
Rep 1 Time:	Rep 2 Time:	Rep 3 Time:	Rep 4 Time:	Rep 5 Time:	
Reps Under Par:		Ave Time:	Total Score:	# of X's:	
Date:	Location:	Weapon:	Sights	Par: 2 Sec / 1.5 Sec	Notes:
Rep 1 Time:	Rep 2 Time:	Rep 3 Time:	Rep 4 Time:	Rep 5 Time:	
Reps Under Par:		Ave Time:	Total Score:	# of X's:	
Date:	Location:	Weapon:	Sights	Par: 2 Sec / 1.5 Sec	Notes:
Rep 1 Time:	Rep 2 Time:	Rep 3 Time:	Rep 4 Time:	Rep 5 Time:	
Reps Under Par:		Ave Time:	Total Score:	# of X's:	

Fundamental Carbine ©

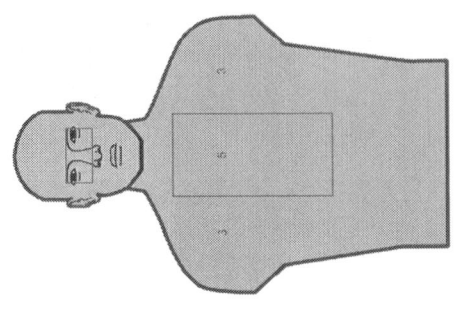

SLEDGE HAMMER

Purpose: Increase competency and accuracy of the use of sustained fire.

Distance: 10 Yards.

Target: JD-QUAL1

Par Time: 1.2 Seconds.

Extra Equipment Needed: Shot timer.

Rounds Fired Per Rep: 2 Rounds.　　**Total Rounds Fired:** 10 Rounds.

Point Penalty: Go or No Go.

Repetitions: 5 Reps.

Starting Position & Condition: Standing - Low Ready. Condition 1.

Description: At the beep of the timer, fire 2 rounds into the A Zone (5 point) body box within 1.2 seconds. The key to this drill is to shoot two flash sight picture shots within the par time, while maintaining good recoil management. Repeat drill 5 times. If any of the repetitions fail to make par time or shots are out of the A Zone (5 point) body box, the drill is a No Go.

Goals: Novice: 1.2 Seconds.　　　　Expert: 1 Second.　　　　Gunfighter: 0.85 Seconds.

Variations: Head shots only. Advanced shooters can add distance.

SLEDGE HAMMER

Date:	Location:	Weapon:	Sights:	Par Goal:
Rep 1 Time:	Rep 2 Time:	Rep 3 Time:	Rep 4 Time:	Rep 5 Time:
Distance:	Body / Head	# of No Go's:	# of Go's:	Average Time:

Date:	Location:	Weapon:	Sights:	Par Goal:
Rep 1 Time:	Rep 2 Time:	Rep 3 Time:	Rep 4 Time:	Rep 5 Time:
Distance:	Body / Head	# of No Go's:	# of Go's:	Average Time:

Date:	Location:	Weapon:	Sights:	Par Goal:
Rep 1 Time:	Rep 2 Time:	Rep 3 Time:	Rep 4 Time:	Rep 5 Time:
Distance:	Body / Head	# of No Go's:	# of Go's:	Average Time:

Date:	Location:	Weapon:	Sights:	Par Goal:
Rep 1 Time:	Rep 2 Time:	Rep 3 Time:	Rep 4 Time:	Rep 5 Time:
Distance:	Body / Head	# of No Go's:	# of Go's:	Average Time:

Date:	Location:	Weapon:	Sights:	Par Goal:
Rep 1 Time:	Rep 2 Time:	Rep 3 Time:	Rep 4 Time:	Rep 5 Time:
Distance:	Body / Head	# of No Go's:	# of Go's:	Average Time:

Fundamental Carbine ©

Recoil Management - 2

SLEDGE HAMMER

Date:	Location:	Weapon:	Sights:	Par Goal:
Rep 1 Time:	Rep 2 Time:	Rep 3 Time:	Rep 4 Time:	Rep 5 Time:
Distance:	Body / Head	# of No Go's:	# of Go's:	Average Time:

Date:	Location:	Weapon:	Sights:	Par Goal:
Rep 1 Time:	Rep 2 Time:	Rep 3 Time:	Rep 4 Time:	Rep 5 Time:
Distance:	Body / Head	# of No Go's:	# of Go's:	Average Time:

Date:	Location:	Weapon:	Sights:	Par Goal:
Rep 1 Time:	Rep 2 Time:	Rep 3 Time:	Rep 4 Time:	Rep 5 Time:
Distance:	Body / Head	# of No Go's:	# of Go's:	Average Time:

Date:	Location:	Weapon:	Sights:	Par Goal:
Rep 1 Time:	Rep 2 Time:	Rep 3 Time:	Rep 4 Time:	Rep 5 Time:
Distance:	Body / Head	# of No Go's:	# of Go's:	Average Time:

Date:	Location:	Weapon:	Sights:	Par Goal:
Rep 1 Time:	Rep 2 Time:	Rep 3 Time:	Rep 4 Time:	Rep 5 Time:
Distance:	Body / Head	# of No Go's:	# of Go's:	Average Time:

www.GUNFIGHTERSERIES.com ©

SLEDGE HAMMER

Date:	Location:	Weapon:	Sights:	Par Goal:
Rep 1 Time:	Rep 2 Time:	Rep 3 Time:	Rep 4 Time:	Rep 5 Time:
Distance:	Body / Head	# of No Go's:	# of Go's:	Average Time:

Date:	Location:	Weapon:	Sights:	Par Goal:
Rep 1 Time:	Rep 2 Time:	Rep 3 Time:	Rep 4 Time:	Rep 5 Time:
Distance:	Body / Head	# of No Go's:	# of Go's:	Average Time:

Date:	Location:	Weapon:	Sights:	Par Goal:
Rep 1 Time:	Rep 2 Time:	Rep 3 Time:	Rep 4 Time:	Rep 5 Time:
Distance:	Body / Head	# of No Go's:	# of Go's:	Average Time:

Date:	Location:	Weapon:	Sights:	Par Goal:
Rep 1 Time:	Rep 2 Time:	Rep 3 Time:	Rep 4 Time:	Rep 5 Time:
Distance:	Body / Head	# of No Go's:	# of Go's:	Average Time:

Date:	Location:	Weapon:	Sights:	Par Goal:
Rep 1 Time:	Rep 2 Time:	Rep 3 Time:	Rep 4 Time:	Rep 5 Time:
Distance:	Body / Head	# of No Go's:	# of Go's:	Average Time:

SLEDGE HAMMER

Date:	Location:	Weapon:	Sights:	Par Goal:
Rep 1 Time:	Rep 2 Time:	Rep 3 Time:	Rep 4 Time:	Rep 5 Time:
Distance:	Body / Head	# of No Go's:	# of Go's:	Average Time:

Date:	Location:	Weapon:	Sights:	Par Goal:
Rep 1 Time:	Rep 2 Time:	Rep 3 Time:	Rep 4 Time:	Rep 5 Time:
Distance:	Body / Head	# of No Go's:	# of Go's:	Average Time:

Date:	Location:	Weapon:	Sights:	Par Goal:
Rep 1 Time:	Rep 2 Time:	Rep 3 Time:	Rep 4 Time:	Rep 5 Time:
Distance:	Body / Head	# of No Go's:	# of Go's:	Average Time:

Date:	Location:	Weapon:	Sights:	Par Goal:
Rep 1 Time:	Rep 2 Time:	Rep 3 Time:	Rep 4 Time:	Rep 5 Time:
Distance:	Body / Head	# of No Go's:	# of Go's:	Average Time:

Date:	Location:	Weapon:	Sights:	Par Goal:
Rep 1 Time:	Rep 2 Time:	Rep 3 Time:	Rep 4 Time:	Rep 5 Time:
Distance:	Body / Head	# of No Go's:	# of Go's:	Average Time:

www.GUNFIGHTERSERIES.com ©

SLEDGE HAMMER

Date:	Location:	Weapon:	Sights:	Par Goal:
Rep 1 Time:	Rep 2 Time:	Rep 3 Time:	Rep 4 Time:	Rep 5 Time:
Distance:	Body / Head	# of No Go's:	# of Go's:	Average Time

Date:	Location:	Weapon:	Sights:	Par Goal:
Rep 1 Time:	Rep 2 Time:	Rep 3 Time:	Rep 4 Time:	Rep 5 Time:
Distance:	Body / Head	# of No Go's:	# of Go's:	Average Time

Date:	Location:	Weapon:	Sights:	Par Goal:
Rep 1 Time:	Rep 2 Time:	Rep 3 Time:	Rep 4 Time:	Rep 5 Time:
Distance:	Body / Head	# of No Go's:	# of Go's:	Average Time

Date:	Location:	Weapon:	Sights:	Par Goal:
Rep 1 Time:	Rep 2 Time:	Rep 3 Time:	Rep 4 Time:	Rep 5 Time:
Distance:	Body / Head	# of No Go's:	# of Go's:	Average Time

Date:	Location:	Weapon:	Sights:	Par Goal:
Rep 1 Time:	Rep 2 Time:	Rep 3 Time:	Rep 4 Time:	Rep 5 Time:
Distance:	Body / Head	# of No Go's:	# of Go's:	Average Time

Recoil Management - 2

Fundamental Carbine ©

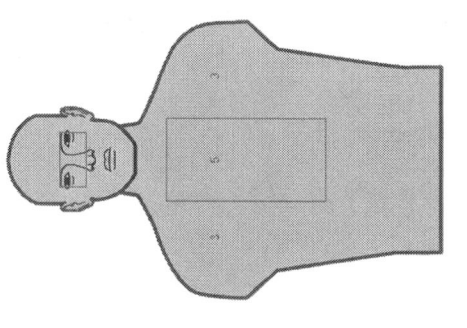

GAS IT

Purpose: Increase consistent shot cadence and shot speed.

Distance: 10 Yards.

Target: JD-QUAL1

Extra Equipment Needed: Shot timer.

Rounds Fired Per Rep: 2 to 5 Rounds / 14 total per rep.

Max Total Rounds Fired: 42 Rounds.

Point Penalty: Go or No Go.

Repetitions: 3 Repetitions of 4 stages.

Starting Position & Condition: Standing - Low Ready. Condition 1.

Description: At the timer beep, aim and fire described number of rounds into the (5 point) A Zone body box with in the listed par time. After you are done firing all of the 4 stages, record your score. Repeat sequence twice more. For highly advanced shooters, put your round in the (5 point) A Zone head box. Goal is all hits in (5 point) A Zone body box and make par time for a given par time set.

Minimum par time	Expert par time	Gunfighter par time
2 rounds 1.8 second par time	2 rounds 1.4 second par time	2 rounds 0.9 second par time
3 rounds 2.3 second par time	3 rounds 1.7 second par time	3 rounds 1.1 second par time
4 rounds 2.8 second par time	4 rounds 2 second par time	4 rounds 1.3 second par time
5 rounds 3.2 second par time	5 rounds 2.3 second par time	5 rounds 1.5 second par time

GAS IT

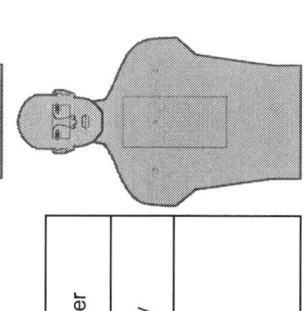

Target 1

Date:	Weapon:	Sights:	Par Time: Novice / Expert / Gunfighter	
Rep 1	2 Shot: Go / No Go	3 Shot: Go / No Go	4 Shot: Go / No Go	5 Shot: Go / No Go	A Box: Head / Body
Rep 2	2 Shot: Go / No Go	3 Shot: Go / No Go	4 Shot: Go / No Go	5 Shot: Go / No Go	Notes:
Rep 3	2 Shot: Go / No Go	3 Shot: Go / No Go	4 Shot: Go / No Go	5 Shot: Go / No Go	

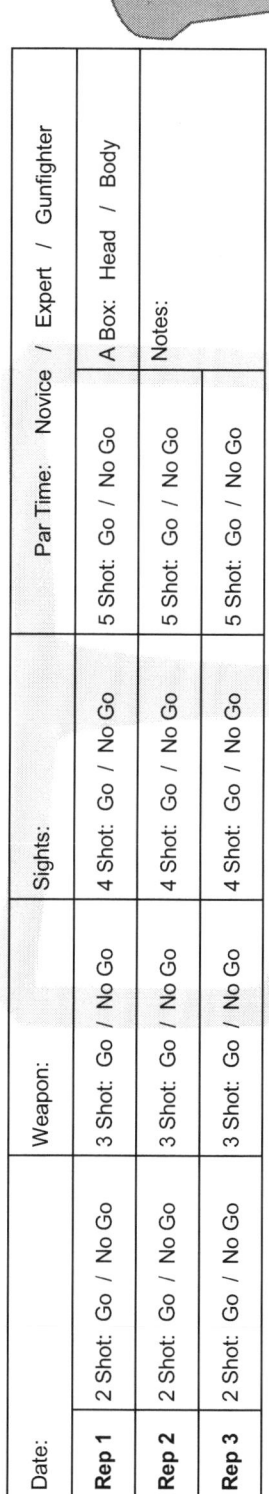

Target 2

Date:	Weapon:	Sights:	Par Time: Novice / Expert / Gunfighter	
Rep 1	2 Shot: Go / No Go	3 Shot: Go / No Go	4 Shot: Go / No Go	5 Shot: Go / No Go	A Box: Head / Body
Rep 2	2 Shot: Go / No Go	3 Shot: Go / No Go	4 Shot: Go / No Go	5 Shot: Go / No Go	Notes:
Rep 3	2 Shot: Go / No Go	3 Shot: Go / No Go	4 Shot: Go / No Go	5 Shot: Go / No Go	

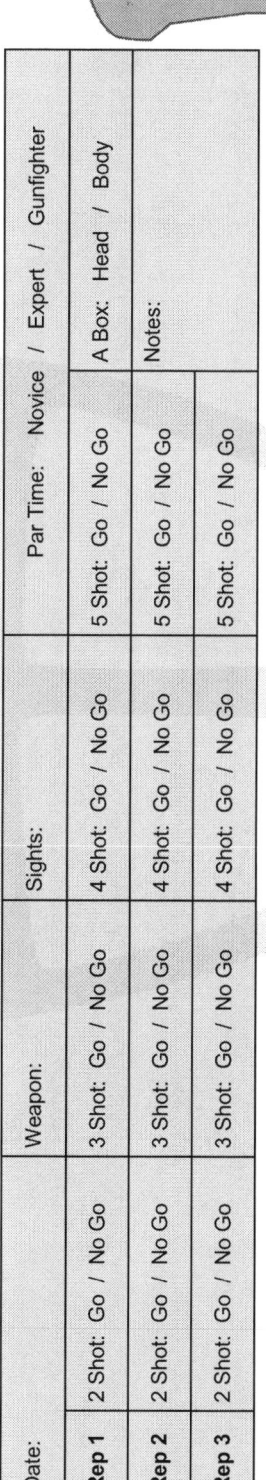

Target 3

Date:	Weapon:	Sights:	Par Time: Novice / Expert / Gunfighter	
Rep 1	2 Shot: Go / No Go	3 Shot: Go / No Go	4 Shot: Go / No Go	5 Shot: Go / No Go	A Box: Head / Body
Rep 2	2 Shot: Go / No Go	3 Shot: Go / No Go	4 Shot: Go / No Go	5 Shot: Go / No Go	Notes:
Rep 3	2 Shot: Go / No Go	3 Shot: Go / No Go	4 Shot: Go / No Go	5 Shot: Go / No Go	

Fundamental Carbine ©

Recoil Management - 3

GAS IT

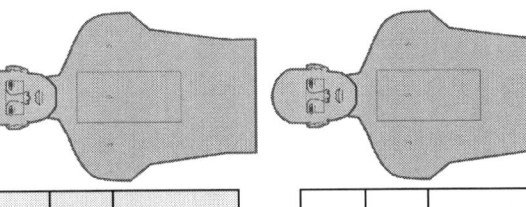

Date:	Weapon:	Sights:	Par Time: Novice / Expert / Gunfighter	A Box: Head / Body
Rep 1	2 Shot: Go / No Go	3 Shot: Go / No Go	4 Shot: Go / No Go	5 Shot: Go / No Go
Rep 2	2 Shot: Go / No Go	3 Shot: Go / No Go	4 Shot: Go / No Go	5 Shot: Go / No Go
Rep 3	2 Shot: Go / No Go	3 Shot: Go / No Go	4 Shot: Go / No Go	5 Shot: Go / No Go

Notes:

Date:	Weapon:	Sights:	Par Time: Novice / Expert / Gunfighter	A Box: Head / Body
Rep 1	2 Shot: Go / No Go	3 Shot: Go / No Go	4 Shot: Go / No Go	5 Shot: Go / No Go
Rep 2	2 Shot: Go / No Go	3 Shot: Go / No Go	4 Shot: Go / No Go	5 Shot: Go / No Go
Rep 3	2 Shot: Go / No Go	3 Shot: Go / No Go	4 Shot: Go / No Go	5 Shot: Go / No Go

Notes:

Date:	Weapon:	Sights:	Par Time: Novice / Expert / Gunfighter	A Box: Head / Body
Rep 1	2 Shot: Go / No Go	3 Shot: Go / No Go	4 Shot: Go / No Go	5 Shot: Go / No Go
Rep 2	2 Shot: Go / No Go	3 Shot: Go / No Go	4 Shot: Go / No Go	5 Shot: Go / No Go
Rep 3	2 Shot: Go / No Go	3 Shot: Go / No Go	4 Shot: Go / No Go	5 Shot: Go / No Go

Notes:

www.GUNFIGHTERSERIES.com ©

GAS IT

Date:	Weapon:	Sights:	Par Time: Novice / Expert / Gunfighter
Rep 1	2 Shot: Go / No Go	3 Shot: Go / No Go	4 Shot: Go / No Go	5 Shot: Go / No Go	A Box: Head / Body
Rep 2	2 Shot: Go / No Go	3 Shot: Go / No Go	4 Shot: Go / No Go	5 Shot: Go / No Go	Notes:
Rep 3	2 Shot: Go / No Go	3 Shot: Go / No Go	4 Shot: Go / No Go	5 Shot: Go / No Go	

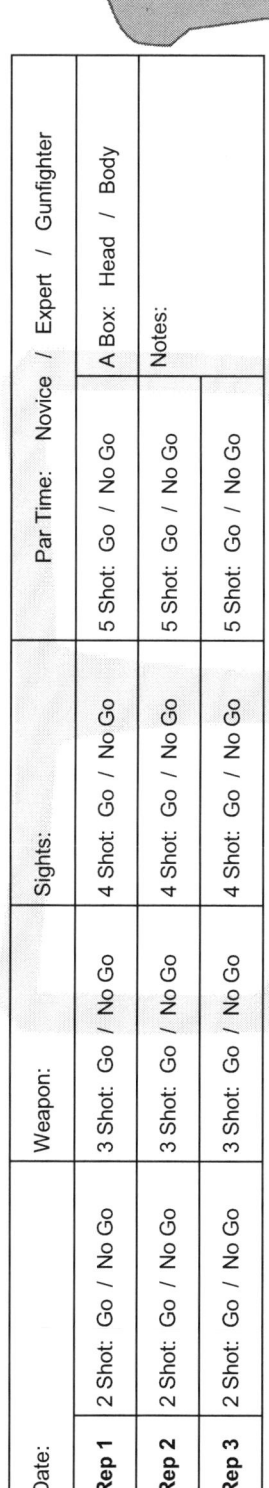

Date:	Weapon:	Sights:	Par Time: Novice / Expert / Gunfighter
Rep 1	2 Shot: Go / No Go	3 Shot: Go / No Go	4 Shot: Go / No Go	5 Shot: Go / No Go	A Box: Head / Body
Rep 2	2 Shot: Go / No Go	3 Shot: Go / No Go	4 Shot: Go / No Go	5 Shot: Go / No Go	Notes:
Rep 3	2 Shot: Go / No Go	3 Shot: Go / No Go	4 Shot: Go / No Go	5 Shot: Go / No Go	

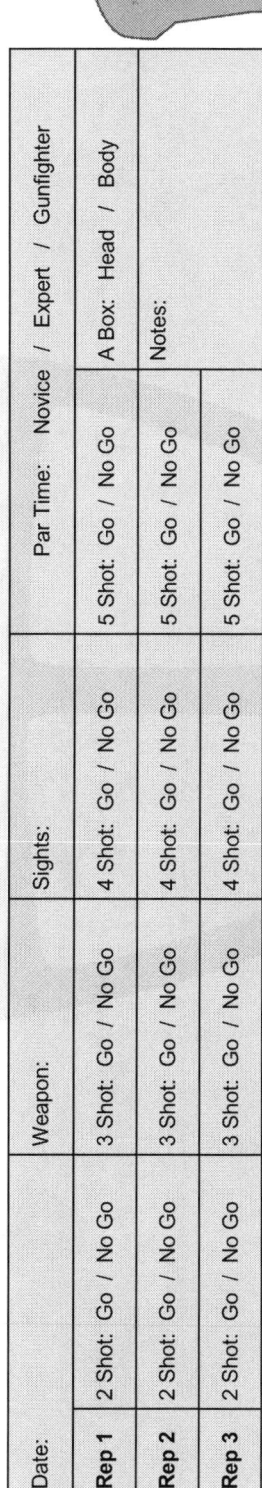

Date:	Weapon:	Sights:	Par Time: Novice / Expert / Gunfighter
Rep 1	2 Shot: Go / No Go	3 Shot: Go / No Go	4 Shot: Go / No Go	5 Shot: Go / No Go	A Box: Head / Body
Rep 2	2 Shot: Go / No Go	3 Shot: Go / No Go	4 Shot: Go / No Go	5 Shot: Go / No Go	Notes:
Rep 3	2 Shot: Go / No Go	3 Shot: Go / No Go	4 Shot: Go / No Go	5 Shot: Go / No Go	

GAS IT

www.GUNFIGHTERSERIES.com ©

Target 1

Date:

Weapon: Sights: Par Time: Novice / Expert / Gunfighter   A Box: Head / Body

Notes:

Rep 1	2 Shot: Go / No Go	3 Shot: Go / No Go	4 Shot: Go / No Go	5 Shot: Go / No Go
Rep 2	2 Shot: Go / No Go	3 Shot: Go / No Go	4 Shot: Go / No Go	5 Shot: Go / No Go
Rep 3	2 Shot: Go / No Go	3 Shot: Go / No Go	4 Shot: Go / No Go	5 Shot: Go / No Go

Target 2

Date:

Weapon: Sights: Par Time: Novice / Expert / Gunfighter   A Box: Head / Body

Notes:

Rep 1	2 Shot: Go / No Go	3 Shot: Go / No Go	4 Shot: Go / No Go	5 Shot: Go / No Go
Rep 2	2 Shot: Go / No Go	3 Shot: Go / No Go	4 Shot: Go / No Go	5 Shot: Go / No Go
Rep 3	2 Shot: Go / No Go	3 Shot: Go / No Go	4 Shot: Go / No Go	5 Shot: Go / No Go

Target 3

Date:

Weapon: Sights: Par Time: Novice / Expert / Gunfighter   A Box: Head / Body

Notes:

Rep 1	2 Shot: Go / No Go	3 Shot: Go / No Go	4 Shot: Go / No Go	5 Shot: Go / No Go
Rep 2	2 Shot: Go / No Go	3 Shot: Go / No Go	4 Shot: Go / No Go	5 Shot: Go / No Go
Rep 3	2 Shot: Go / No Go	3 Shot: Go / No Go	4 Shot: Go / No Go	5 Shot: Go / No Go

GAS IT

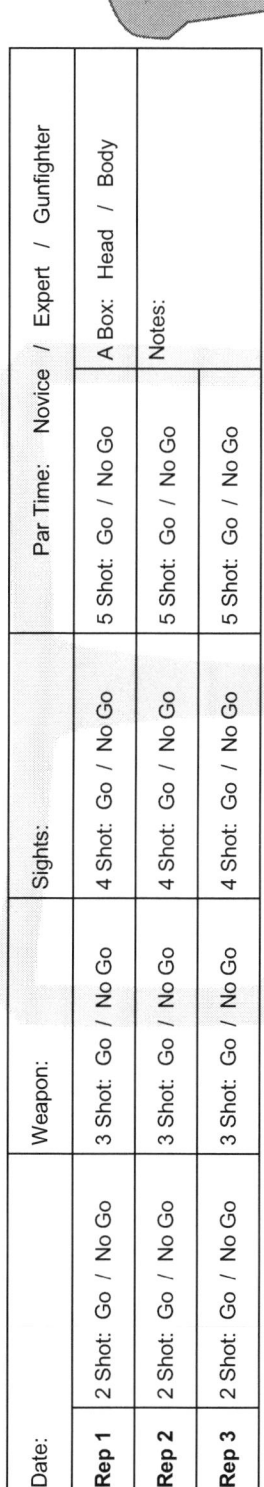
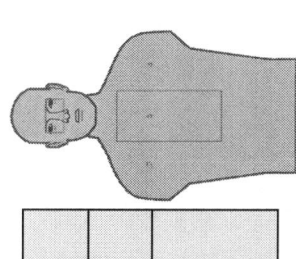
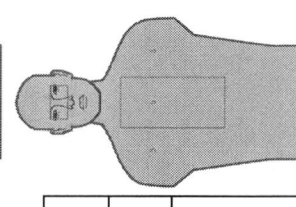

Date:	**Weapon:**	**Sights:**	**Par Time:** Novice / Expert / Gunfighter	**A Box:** Head / Body
Rep 1	2 Shot: Go / No Go	3 Shot: Go / No Go	4 Shot: Go / No Go	5 Shot: Go / No Go	**Notes:**
Rep 2	2 Shot: Go / No Go	3 Shot: Go / No Go	4 Shot: Go / No Go	5 Shot: Go / No Go
Rep 3	2 Shot: Go / No Go	3 Shot: Go / No Go	4 Shot: Go / No Go	5 Shot: Go / No Go

Date:	**Weapon:**	**Sights:**	**Par Time:** Novice / Expert / Gunfighter	**A Box:** Head / Body
Rep 1	2 Shot: Go / No Go	3 Shot: Go / No Go	4 Shot: Go / No Go	5 Shot: Go / No Go	**Notes:**
Rep 2	2 Shot: Go / No Go	3 Shot: Go / No Go	4 Shot: Go / No Go	5 Shot: Go / No Go
Rep 3	2 Shot: Go / No Go	3 Shot: Go / No Go	4 Shot: Go / No Go	5 Shot: Go / No Go

Date:	**Weapon:**	**Sights:**	**Par Time:** Novice / Expert / Gunfighter	**A Box:** Head / Body
Rep 1	2 Shot: Go / No Go	3 Shot: Go / No Go	4 Shot: Go / No Go	5 Shot: Go / No Go	**Notes:**
Rep 2	2 Shot: Go / No Go	3 Shot: Go / No Go	4 Shot: Go / No Go	5 Shot: Go / No Go
Rep 3	2 Shot: Go / No Go	3 Shot: Go / No Go	4 Shot: Go / No Go	5 Shot: Go / No Go

CADENCE COUNT

Purpose: Increase accuracy under recoil management while forcing shooter to think.

Distance: 15 Yards.

Target: GF-1

Par Time: 15 Seconds.

Extra Equipment Needed: Shot timer.

Rounds Fired Per Rep: 15 Rounds.

Point Penalty: As per target score.

Starting Position & Condition: Standing - Low Ready. Condition 1 with more than 15 rounds in magazine.

Description: At the timer beep, fire 15 rounds into the target within 15 seconds. The goal of this drill is to keep a minimum of all of the rounds in the black of the target equaling 145 points. You will need to count your number of shots to not make this drill a failure.

Goals: Novice: 135 Points.   Expert: 150 Points.   Gunfighter: 150 Points - 10X

Variations: Start with any ready position you choose.

CADENCE COUNT

Date:	Location:	Weapon:	Sights:
# of 8's:	# of 9's:	# of 10's:	Total Score:	X's:
Total # of shots:	Shots over par:	Notes:		

Date:	Location:	Weapon:	Sights:
# of 8's:	# of 9's:	# of 10's:	Total Score:	X's:
Total # of shots:	Shots over par:	Notes:		

Date:	Location:	Weapon:	Sights:
# of 8's:	# of 9's:	# of 10's:	Total Score:	X's:
Total # of shots:	Shots over par:	Notes:		

Date:	Location:	Weapon:	Sights:
# of 8's:	# of 9's:	# of 10's:	Total Score:	X's:
Total # of shots:	Shots over par:	Notes:		

Date:	Location:	Weapon:	Sights:
# of 8's:	# of 9's:	# of 10's:	Total Score:	X's:
Total # of shot:	Shots over par:	Notes:		

CADENCE COUNT

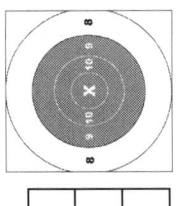 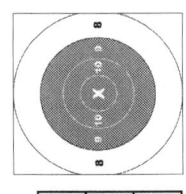 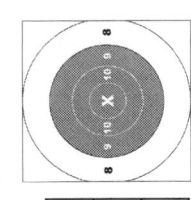 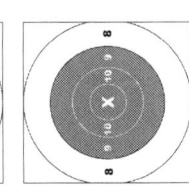 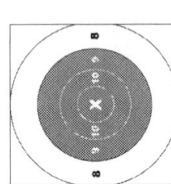

Date:	Location:	Weapon:	Sights:
# of 8's:	# of 9's:	# of 10's:	Total Score: X's:
Total # of shots:	Shots over par:	Notes:	

Date:	Location:	Weapon:	Sights:
# of 8's:	# of 9's:	# of 10's:	Total Score: X's:
Total # of shots:	Shots over par:	Notes:	

Date:	Location:	Weapon:	Sights:
# of 8's:	# of 9's:	# of 10's:	Total Score: X's:
Total # of shots:	Shots over par:	Notes:	

Date:	Location:	Weapon:	Sights:
# of 8's:	# of 9's:	# of 10's:	Total Score: X's:
Total # of shots:	Shots over par:	Notes:	

Date:	Location:	Weapon:	Sights:
# of 8's:	# of 9's:	# of 10's:	Total Score: X's:
Total # of shot:	Shots over par:	Notes:	

CADENCE COUNT

Date:	Location:	Weapon:	Sights:
# of 8's:	# of 9's:	# of 10's:	**Total Score:** X's:
Total # of shots:	Shots over par:	Notes:	

Date:	Location:	Weapon:	Sights:
# of 8's:	# of 9's:	# of 10's:	**Total Score:** X's:
Total # of shots:	Shots over par:	Notes:	

Date:	Location:	Weapon:	Sights:
# of 8's:	# of 9's:	# of 10's:	**Total Score:** X's:
Total # of shots:	Shots over par:	Notes:	

Date:	Location:	Weapon:	Sights:
# of 8's:	# of 9's:	# of 10's:	**Total Score:** X's:
Total # of shots:	Shots over par:	Notes:	

Date:	Location:	Weapon:	Sights:
# of 8's:	# of 9's:	# of 10's:	**Total Score:** X's:
Total # of shot:	Shots over par:	Notes:	

Recoil Management - 4

Fundamental Carbine ©

CADENCE COUNT

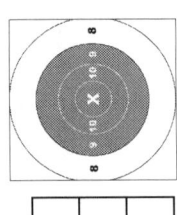 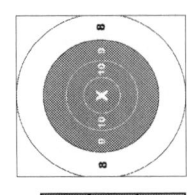 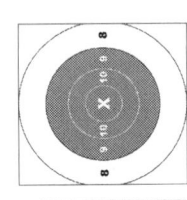 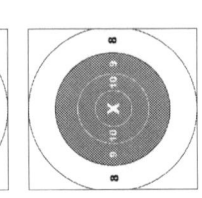 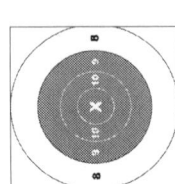

Date:	Location:	Weapon:	Sights:
# of 8's:	# of 9's:	# of 10's:	Total Score: X's:
Total # of shots:	Shots over par:	Notes:	

Date:	Location:	Weapon:	Sights:
# of 8's:	# of 9's:	# of 10's:	Total Score: X's:
Total # of shots:	Shots over par:	Notes:	

Date:	Location:	Weapon:	Sights:
# of 8's:	# of 9's:	# of 10's:	Total Score: X's:
Total # of shots:	Shots over par:	Notes:	

Date:	Location:	Weapon:	Sights:
# of 8's:	# of 9's:	# of 10's:	Total Score: X's:
Total # of shots:	Shots over par:	Notes:	

Date:	Location:	Weapon:	Sights:
# of 8's:	# of 9's:	# of 10's:	Total Score: X's:
Total # of shot:	Shots over par:	Notes:	

CADENCE COUNT

Date:	Location:	Weapon:	Sights:
# of 8's:	# of 9's:	# of 10's:	Total Score:	X's:
Total # of shots:	Shots over par:	Notes:	

Date:	Location:	Weapon:	Sights:
# of 8's:	# of 9's:	# of 10's:	Total Score:	X's:
Total # of shots:	Shots over par:	Notes:	

Date:	Location:	Weapon:	Sights:
# of 8's:	# of 9's:	# of 10's:	Total Score:	X's:
Total # of shots:	Shots over par:	Notes:	

Date:	Location:	Weapon:	Sights:
# of 8's:	# of 9's:	# of 10's:	Total Score:	X's:
Total # of shots:	Shots over par:	Notes:	

Date:	Location:	Weapon:	Sights:
# of 8's:	# of 9's:	# of 10's:	Total Score:	X's:
Total # of shot:	Shots over par:	Notes:	

Recoil Management - 4

Fundamental Carbine ©

PRONE OUT

Purpose: Increase the accuracy and competency of the prone position.

Distance: 100 Yards.

Target: JD-QUAL1

Par Time: 15 Seconds.

Extra Equipment Needed: Shot timer. Spotting scope (optional).

Rounds Fired Per Rep: 3 Rounds.   **Total Rounds Fired:** 15 Rounds.

Point Penalty: As per target score.

Repetitions: 5 Reps.

Starting Position & Condition: Standing - Any ready position you choose to prone. Condition 1.

Description: At the timer beep, go to the prone position while keeping the carbine pointed down range at the targets direction. Take aim at the target and fire 3 rounds into the A Zone (5 point) body or head box. Record how many times you made par time and hit within the A Zone (5 point) body or head box. Not making par time and/or not making ther minimum goal points makes the drill a failure.

Goals: Novice: 45 Points within par.   Expert: 67 Points within par.   Gunfighter: 75 Points within par.

PRONE OUT

Date:	Location:	Weapon:	Sights:	Body / Head	Notes:
Rep 1 Time:	Rep 2 Time:	Rep 3 Time:	Rep 4 Time:	Rep 5 Time:	
Rep 1 Score:	Rep 2 Score:	Rep 3 Score:	Rep 4 Score:	Rep 5 Score:	**Total Score:**

Date:	Location:	Weapon:	Sights:	Body / Head	Notes:
Rep 1 Time:	Rep 2 Time:	Rep 3 Time:	Rep 4 Time:	Rep 5 Time:	
Rep 1 Score:	Rep 2 Score:	Rep 3 Score:	Rep 4 Score:	Rep 5 Score:	**Total Score:**

Date:	Location:	Weapon:	Sights:	Body / Head	Notes:
Rep 1 Time:	Rep 2 Time:	Rep 3 Time:	Rep 4 Time:	Rep 5 Time:	
Rep 1 Score:	Rep 2 Score:	Rep 3 Score:	Rep 4 Score:	Rep 5 Score:	**Total Score:**

Date:	Location:	Weapon:	Sights:	Body / Head	Notes:
Rep 1 Time:	Rep 2 Time:	Rep 3 Time:	Rep 4 Time:	Rep 5 Time:	
Rep 1 Score:	Rep 2 Score:	Rep 3 Score:	Rep 4 Score:	Rep 5 Score:	**Total Score:**

Date:	Location:	Weapon:	Sights:	Body / Head	Notes:
Rep 1 Time:	Rep 2 Time:	Rep 3 Time:	Rep 4 Time:	Rep 5 Time:	
Rep 1 Score:	Rep 2 Score:	Rep 3 Score:	Rep 4 Score:	Rep 5 Score:	**Total Score:**

Positions - 1

Fundamental Carbine ©

PRONE OUT

Date:	Location:	Weapon:	Sights:	Body / Head	Notes:
Rep 1 Time:	Rep 2 Time:	Rep 3 Time:	Rep 4 Time:	Rep 5 Time:	
Rep 1 Score:	Rep 2 Score:	Rep 3 Score:	Rep 4 Score:	Rep 5 Score:	**Total Score:**

Date:	Location:	Weapon:	Sights:	Body / Head	Notes:
Rep 1 Time:	Rep 2 Time:	Rep 3 Time:	Rep 4 Time:	Rep 5 Time:	
Rep 1 Score:	Rep 2 Score:	Rep 3 Score:	Rep 4 Score:	Rep 5 Score:	**Total Score:**

Date:	Location:	Weapon:	Sights:	Body / Head	Notes:
Rep 1 Time:	Rep 2 Time:	Rep 3 Time:	Rep 4 Time:	Rep 5 Time:	
Rep 1 Score:	Rep 2 Score:	Rep 3 Score:	Rep 4 Score:	Rep 5 Score:	**Total Score:**

Date:	Location:	Weapon:	Sights:	Body / Head	Notes:
Rep 1 Time:	Rep 2 Time:	Rep 3 Time:	Rep 4 Time:	Rep 5 Time:	
Rep 1 Score:	Rep 2 Score:	Rep 3 Score:	Rep 4 Score:	Rep 5 Score:	**Total Score:**

Date:	Location:	Weapon:	Sights:	Body / Head	Notes:
Rep 1 Time:	Rep 2 Time:	Rep 3 Time:	Rep 4 Time:	Rep 5 Time:	
Rep 1 Score:	Rep 2 Score:	Rep 3 Score:	Rep 4 Score:	Rep 5 Score:	**Total Score:**

PRONE OUT

Date:	Location:	Weapon:	Sights:	Body / Head	Notes:
Rep 1 Time:	Rep 2 Time:	Rep 3 Time:	Rep 4 Time:	Rep 5 Time:	
Rep 1 Score:	Rep 2 Score:	Rep 3 Score:	Rep 4 Score:	Rep 5 Score:	**Total Score:**

Date:	Location:	Weapon:	Sights:	Body / Head	Notes:
Rep 1 Time:	Rep 2 Time:	Rep 3 Time:	Rep 4 Time:	Rep 5 Time:	
Rep 1 Score:	Rep 2 Score:	Rep 3 Score:	Rep 4 Score:	Rep 5 Score:	**Total Score:**

Date:	Location:	Weapon:	Sights:	Body / Head	Notes:
Rep 1 Time:	Rep 2 Time:	Rep 3 Time:	Rep 4 Time:	Rep 5 Time:	
Rep 1 Score:	Rep 2 Score:	Rep 3 Score:	Rep 4 Score:	Rep 5 Score:	**Total Score:**

Date:	Location:	Weapon:	Sights:	Body / Head	Notes:
Rep 1 Time:	Rep 2 Time:	Rep 3 Time:	Rep 4 Time:	Rep 5 Time:	
Rep 1 Score:	Rep 2 Score:	Rep 3 Score:	Rep 4 Score:	Rep 5 Score:	**Total Score:**

Date:	Location:	Weapon:	Sights:	Body / Head	Notes:
Rep 1 Time:	Rep 2 Time:	Rep 3 Time:	Rep 4 Time:	Rep 5 Time:	
Rep 1 Score:	Rep 2 Score:	Rep 3 Score:	Rep 4 Score:	Rep 5 Score:	**Total Score:**

Positions - 1

Fundamental Carbine ©

PRONE OUT

Date:	Location:	Weapon:	Sights:	Body / Head	Notes:
Rep 1 Time:	Rep 2 Time:	Rep 3 Time:	Rep 4 Time:	Rep 5 Time:	
Rep 1 Score:	Rep 2 Score:	Rep 3 Score:	Rep 4 Score:	Rep 5 Score:	**Total Score:**

Date:	Location:	Weapon:	Sights:	Body / Head	Notes:
Rep 1 Time:	Rep 2 Time:	Rep 3 Time:	Rep 4 Time:	Rep 5 Time:	
Rep 1 Score:	Rep 2 Score:	Rep 3 Score:	Rep 4 Score:	Rep 5 Score:	**Total Score:**

Date:	Location:	Weapon:	Sights:	Body / Head	Notes:
Rep 1 Time:	Rep 2 Time:	Rep 3 Time:	Rep 4 Time:	Rep 5 Time:	
Rep 1 Score:	Rep 2 Score:	Rep 3 Score:	Rep 4 Score:	Rep 5 Score:	**Total Score:**

Date:	Location:	Weapon:	Sights:	Body / Head	Notes:
Rep 1 Time:	Rep 2 Time:	Rep 3 Time:	Rep 4 Time:	Rep 5 Time:	
Rep 1 Score:	Rep 2 Score:	Rep 3 Score:	Rep 4 Score:	Rep 5 Score:	**Total Score:**

Date:	Location:	Weapon:	Sights:	Body / Head	Notes:
Rep 1 Time:	Rep 2 Time:	Rep 3 Time:	Rep 4 Time:	Rep 5 Time:	
Rep 1 Score:	Rep 2 Score:	Rep 3 Score:	Rep 4 Score:	Rep 5 Score:	**Total Score:**

PRONE OUT

Date:	Location:	Weapon:	Sights:	Body / Head	Notes:
Rep 1 Time:	Rep 2 Time:	Rep 3 Time:	Rep 4 Time:	Rep 5 Time:	
Rep 1 Score:	Rep 2 Score:	Rep 3 Score:	Rep 4 Score:	Rep 5 Score:	**Total Score:**

Date:	Location:	Weapon:	Sights:	Body / Head	Notes:
Rep 1 Time:	Rep 2 Time:	Rep 3 Time:	Rep 4 Time:	Rep 5 Time:	
Rep 1 Score:	Rep 2 Score:	Rep 3 Score:	Rep 4 Score:	Rep 5 Score:	**Total Score:**

Date:	Location:	Weapon:	Sights:	Body / Head	Notes:
Rep 1 Time:	Rep 2 Time:	Rep 3 Time:	Rep 4 Time:	Rep 5 Time:	
Rep 1 Score:	Rep 2 Score:	Rep 3 Score:	Rep 4 Score:	Rep 5 Score:	**Total Score:**

Date:	Location:	Weapon:	Sights:	Body / Head	Notes:
Rep 1 Time:	Rep 2 Time:	Rep 3 Time:	Rep 4 Time:	Rep 5 Time:	
Rep 1 Score:	Rep 2 Score:	Rep 3 Score:	Rep 4 Score:	Rep 5 Score:	**Total Score:**

Date:	Location:	Weapon:	Sights:	Body / Head	Notes:
Rep 1 Time:	Rep 2 Time:	Rep 3 Time:	Rep 4 Time:	Rep 5 Time:	
Rep 1 Score:	Rep 2 Score:	Rep 3 Score:	Rep 4 Score:	Rep 5 Score:	**Total Score:**

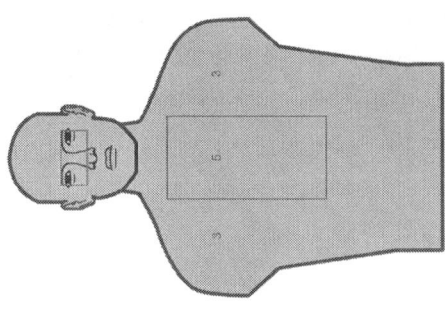

TAKE A KNEE

Purpose: Increase the accuracy and competency of the kneeling position.

Distance: 75 Yards.

Target: JD-QUAL1

Par Time: 12 Seconds.

Extra Equipment Needed: Shot timer. Spotting scope (optional).

Rounds Fired Per Rep: 3 Rounds.   **Total Rounds Fired:** 15 Rounds.

Point Penalty: As per target score.

Repetitions: 5 Reps.

Starting Position & Condition: Standing - Any ready position you choose. Condition 1.

Description: At the timer beep, go to the kneeling position while keeping the carbine pointed down range at the targets direction. Take aim at the target and fire 3 rounds into the A Zone (5 point) body or head box. Record how many times you made par time and hit within the A Zone (5 point) body or head box. Not making par time and/or not making the minimum goal points makes the drill a failure.

Goals: Novice: 45 Points within par.   Expert: 67 Points within par.   Gunfighter: 75 Points within par.

TAKE A KNEE

Date:	Location:	Weapon:	Sights:	Body / Head	Notes:
Rep 1 Time:	Rep 2 Time:	Rep 3 Time:	Rep 4 Time:	Rep 5 Time:	
Rep 1 Score:	Rep 2 Score:	Rep 3 Score:	Rep 4 Score:	Rep 5 Score:	**Total Score:**

Date:	Location:	Weapon:	Sights:	Body / Head	Notes:
Rep 1 Time:	Rep 2 Time:	Rep 3 Time:	Rep 4 Time:	Rep 5 Time:	
Rep 1 Score:	Rep 2 Score:	Rep 3 Score:	Rep 4 Score:	Rep 5 Score:	**Total Score:**

Date:	Location:	Weapon:	Sights:	Body / Head	Notes:
Rep 1 Time:	Rep 2 Time:	Rep 3 Time:	Rep 4 Time:	Rep 5 Time:	
Rep 1 Score:	Rep 2 Score:	Rep 3 Score:	Rep 4 Score:	Rep 5 Score:	**Total Score:**

Date:	Location:	Weapon:	Sights:	Body / Head	Notes:
Rep 1 Time:	Rep 2 Time:	Rep 3 Time:	Rep 4 Time:	Rep 5 Time:	
Rep 1 Score:	Rep 2 Score:	Rep 3 Score:	Rep 4 Score:	Rep 5 Score:	**Total Score:**

Date:	Location:	Weapon:	Sights:	Body / Head	Notes:
Rep 1 Time:	Rep 2 Time:	Rep 3 Time:	Rep 4 Time:	Rep 5 Time:	
Rep 1 Score:	Rep 2 Score:	Rep 3 Score:	Rep 4 Score:	Rep 5 Score:	**Total Score:**

TAKE A KNEE

Date:	Location:	Weapon:	Sights:	Body / Head	Notes:
Rep 1 Time:	Rep 2 Time:	Rep 3 Time:	Rep 4 Time:	Rep 5 Time:	
Rep 1 Score:	Rep 2 Score:	Rep 3 Score:	Rep 4 Score:	Rep 5 Score:	**Total Score:**

Date:	Location:	Weapon:	Sights:	Body / Head	Notes:
Rep 1 Time:	Rep 2 Time:	Rep 3 Time:	Rep 4 Time:	Rep 5 Time:	
Rep 1 Score:	Rep 2 Score:	Rep 3 Score:	Rep 4 Score:	Rep 5 Score:	**Total Score:**

Date:	Location:	Weapon:	Sights:	Body / Head	Notes:
Rep 1 Time:	Rep 2 Time:	Rep 3 Time:	Rep 4 Time:	Rep 5 Time:	
Rep 1 Score:	Rep 2 Score:	Rep 3 Score:	Rep 4 Score:	Rep 5 Score:	**Total Score:**

Date:	Location:	Weapon:	Sights:	Body / Head	Notes:
Rep 1 Time:	Rep 2 Time:	Rep 3 Time:	Rep 4 Time:	Rep 5 Time:	
Rep 1 Score:	Rep 2 Score:	Rep 3 Score:	Rep 4 Score:	Rep 5 Score:	**Total Score:**

Date:	Location:	Weapon:	Sights:	Body / Head	Notes:
Rep 1 Time:	Rep 2 Time:	Rep 3 Time:	Rep 4 Time:	Rep 5 Time:	
Rep 1 Score:	Rep 2 Score:	Rep 3 Score:	Rep 4 Score:	Rep 5 Score:	**Total Score:**

TAKE A KNEE

Date:	Location:	Weapon:	Sights:	Body / Head	Notes:
Rep 1 Time:	Rep 2 Time:	Rep 3 Time:	Rep 4 Time:	Rep 5 Time:	
Rep 1 Score:	Rep 2 Score:	Rep 3 Score:	Rep 4 Score:	Rep 5 Score:	**Total Score:**

Date:	Location:	Weapon:	Sights:	Body / Head	Notes:
Rep 1 Time:	Rep 2 Time:	Rep 3 Time:	Rep 4 Time:	Rep 5 Time:	
Rep 1 Score:	Rep 2 Score:	Rep 3 Score:	Rep 4 Score:	Rep 5 Score:	**Total Score:**

Date:	Location:	Weapon:	Sights:	Body / Head	Notes:
Rep 1 Time:	Rep 2 Time:	Rep 3 Time:	Rep 4 Time:	Rep 5 Time:	
Rep 1 Score:	Rep 2 Score:	Rep 3 Score:	Rep 4 Score:	Rep 5 Score:	**Total Score:**

Date:	Location:	Weapon:	Sights:	Body / Head	Notes:
Rep 1 Time:	Rep 2 Time:	Rep 3 Time:	Rep 4 Time:	Rep 5 Time:	
Rep 1 Score:	Rep 2 Score:	Rep 3 Score:	Rep 4 Score:	Rep 5 Score:	**Total Score:**

Date:	Location:	Weapon:	Sights:	Body / Head	Notes:
Rep 1 Time:	Rep 2 Time:	Rep 3 Time:	Rep 4 Time:	Rep 5 Time:	
Rep 1 Score:	Rep 2 Score:	Rep 3 Score:	Rep 4 Score:	Rep 5 Score:	**Total Score:**

Fundamental Carbine ©

TAKE A KNEE

Date:	Location:	Weapon:	Sights:	Body / Head	Notes:
Rep 1 Time:	Rep 2 Time:	Rep 3 Time:	Rep 4 Time:	Rep 5 Time:	
Rep 1 Score:	Rep 2 Score:	Rep 3 Score:	Rep 4 Score:	Rep 5 Score:	Total Score:

Date:	Location:	Weapon:	Sights:	Body / Head	Notes:
Rep 1 Time:	Rep 2 Time:	Rep 3 Time:	Rep 4 Time:	Rep 5 Time:	
Rep 1 Score:	Rep 2 Score:	Rep 3 Score:	Rep 4 Score:	Rep 5 Score:	Total Score:

Date:	Location:	Weapon:	Sights:	Body / Head	Notes:
Rep 1 Time:	Rep 2 Time:	Rep 3 Time:	Rep 4 Time:	Rep 5 Time:	
Rep 1 Score:	Rep 2 Score:	Rep 3 Score:	Rep 4 Score:	Rep 5 Score:	Total Score:

Date:	Location:	Weapon:	Sights:	Body / Head	Notes:
Rep 1 Time:	Rep 2 Time:	Rep 3 Time:	Rep 4 Time:	Rep 5 Time:	
Rep 1 Score:	Rep 2 Score:	Rep 3 Score:	Rep 4 Score:	Rep 5 Score:	Total Score:

Date:	Location:	Weapon:	Sights:	Body / Head	Notes:
Rep 1 Time:	Rep 2 Time:	Rep 3 Time:	Rep 4 Time:	Rep 5 Time:	
Rep 1 Score:	Rep 2 Score:	Rep 3 Score:	Rep 4 Score:	Rep 5 Score:	Total Score:

www.GUNFIGHTERSERIES.com ©

TAKE A KNEE

Date:	Location:	Weapon:	Sights:	Body / Head	Notes:
Rep 1 Time:	Rep 2 Time:	Rep 3 Time:	Rep 4 Time:	Rep 5 Time:	
Rep 1 Score:	Rep 2 Score:	Rep 3 Score:	Rep 4 Score:	Rep 5 Score:	**Total Score:**

Date:	Location:	Weapon:	Sights:	Body / Head	Notes:
Rep 1 Time:	Rep 2 Time:	Rep 3 Time:	Rep 4 Time:	Rep 5 Time:	
Rep 1 Score:	Rep 2 Score:	Rep 3 Score:	Rep 4 Score:	Rep 5 Score:	**Total Score:**

Date:	Location:	Weapon:	Sights:	Body / Head	Notes:
Rep 1 Time:	Rep 2 Time:	Rep 3 Time:	Rep 4 Time:	Rep 5 Time:	
Rep 1 Score:	Rep 2 Score:	Rep 3 Score:	Rep 4 Score:	Rep 5 Score:	**Total Score:**

Date:	Location:	Weapon:	Sights:	Body / Head	Notes:
Rep 1 Time:	Rep 2 Time:	Rep 3 Time:	Rep 4 Time:	Rep 5 Time:	
Rep 1 Score:	Rep 2 Score:	Rep 3 Score:	Rep 4 Score:	Rep 5 Score:	**Total Score:**

Date:	Location:	Weapon:	Sights:	Body / Head	Notes:
Rep 1 Time:	Rep 2 Time:	Rep 3 Time:	Rep 4 Time:	Rep 5 Time:	
Rep 1 Score:	Rep 2 Score:	Rep 3 Score:	Rep 4 Score:	Rep 5 Score:	**Total Score:**

Fundamental Carbine ©

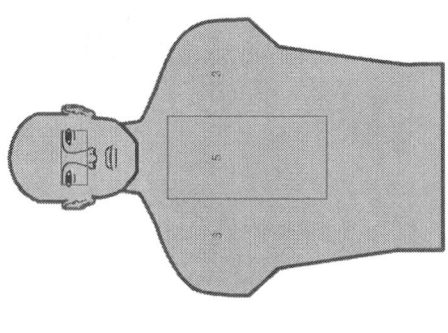

STAND YOUR GROUND

Purpose: Increase the accuracy and competency of the standing position.

Distance: 50 Yards.

Target: JD-QUAL1

Par Time: 8 Seconds.

Extra Equipment Needed: Shot timer. Spotting scope (optional).

Rounds Fired Per Rep: 3 Rounds.   **Total Rounds Fired:** 15 Rounds.

Point Penalty: As per target score.

Repetitions: 5 Reps.

Starting Position & Condition: Standing - Any ready position you choose. Condition 1.

Description: At the timer beep, take aim at the target and fire 3 rounds into the A Zone (5 point) body or head box. Record how many times you made par time and hit within the A Zone (5 point) body or head box. Not making par time and/or not making the minimum goal points makes the drill a failure.

Goals: Novice: 45 Points within par.   Expert: 67 Points within par.   Gunfighter: 75 Points within par.

STAND YOUR GROUND

Date:	Location:	Weapon:	Sights:	Body / Head	Notes:
Rep 1 Time:	Rep 2 Time:	Rep 3 Time:	Rep 4 Time:	Rep 5 Time:	
Rep 1 Score:	Rep 2 Score:	Rep 3 Score:	Rep 4 Score:	Rep 5 Score:	**Total Score:**

Date:	Location:	Weapon:	Sights:	Body / Head	Notes:
Rep 1 Time:	Rep 2 Time:	Rep 3 Time:	Rep 4 Time:	Rep 5 Time:	
Rep 1 Score:	Rep 2 Score:	Rep 3 Score:	Rep 4 Score:	Rep 5 Score:	**Total Score:**

Date:	Location:	Weapon:	Sights:	Body / Head	Notes:
Rep 1 Time:	Rep 2 Time:	Rep 3 Time:	Rep 4 Time:	Rep 5 Time:	
Rep 1 Score:	Rep 2 Score:	Rep 3 Score:	Rep 4 Score:	Rep 5 Score:	**Total Score:**

Date:	Location:	Weapon:	Sights:	Body / Head	Notes:
Rep 1 Time:	Rep 2 Time:	Rep 3 Time:	Rep 4 Time:	Rep 5 Time:	
Rep 1 Score:	Rep 2 Score:	Rep 3 Score:	Rep 4 Score:	Rep 5 Score:	**Total Score:**

Date:	Location:	Weapon:	Sights:	Body / Head	Notes:
Rep 1 Time:	Rep 2 Time:	Rep 3 Time:	Rep 4 Time:	Rep 5 Time:	
Rep 1 Score:	Rep 2 Score:	Rep 3 Score:	Rep 4 Score:	Rep 5 Score:	**Total Score:**

STAND YOUR GROUND

Date:	Location:	Weapon:	Sights:	Body / Head	Notes:
Rep 1 Time:	Rep 2 Time:	Rep 3 Time:	Rep 4 Time:	Rep 5 Time:	
Rep 1 Score:	Rep 2 Score:	Rep 3 Score:	Rep 4 Score:	Rep 5 Score:	**Total Score:**

Date:	Location:	Weapon:	Sights:	Body / Head	Notes:
Rep 1 Time:	Rep 2 Time:	Rep 3 Time:	Rep 4 Time:	Rep 5 Time:	
Rep 1 Score:	Rep 2 Score:	Rep 3 Score:	Rep 4 Score:	Rep 5 Score:	**Total Score:**

Date:	Location:	Weapon:	Sights:	Body / Head	Notes:
Rep 1 Time:	Rep 2 Time:	Rep 3 Time:	Rep 4 Time:	Rep 5 Time:	
Rep 1 Score:	Rep 2 Score:	Rep 3 Score:	Rep 4 Score:	Rep 5 Score:	**Total Score:**

Date:	Location:	Weapon:	Sights:	Body / Head	Notes:
Rep 1 Time:	Rep 2 Time:	Rep 3 Time:	Rep 4 Time:	Rep 5 Time:	
Rep 1 Score:	Rep 2 Score:	Rep 3 Score:	Rep 4 Score:	Rep 5 Score:	**Total Score:**

Date:	Location:	Weapon:	Sights:	Body / Head	Notes:
Rep 1 Time:	Rep 2 Time:	Rep 3 Time:	Rep 4 Time:	Rep 5 Time:	
Rep 1 Score:	Rep 2 Score:	Rep 3 Score:	Rep 4 Score:	Rep 5 Score:	**Total Score:**

STAND YOUR GROUND

Date:	Location:	Weapon:	Sights:	Body / Head	Notes:
Rep 1 Time:	Rep 2 Time:	Rep 3 Time:	Rep 4 Time:	Rep 5 Time:	
Rep 1 Score:	Rep 2 Score:	Rep 3 Score:	Rep 4 Score:	Rep 5 Score:	**Total Score:**

Date:	Location:	Weapon:	Sights:	Body / Head	Notes:
Rep 1 Time:	Rep 2 Time:	Rep 3 Time:	Rep 4 Time:	Rep 5 Time:	
Rep 1 Score:	Rep 2 Score:	Rep 3 Score:	Rep 4 Score:	Rep 5 Score:	**Total Score:**

Date:	Location:	Weapon:	Sights:	Body / Head	Notes:
Rep 1 Time:	Rep 2 Time:	Rep 3 Time:	Rep 4 Time:	Rep 5 Time:	
Rep 1 Score:	Rep 2 Score:	Rep 3 Score:	Rep 4 Score:	Rep 5 Score:	**Total Score:**

Date:	Location:	Weapon:	Sights:	Body / Head	Notes:
Rep 1 Time:	Rep 2 Time:	Rep 3 Time:	Rep 4 Time:	Rep 5 Time:	
Rep 1 Score:	Rep 2 Score:	Rep 3 Score:	Rep 4 Score:	Rep 5 Score:	**Total Score:**

Date:	Location:	Weapon:	Sights:	Body / Head	Notes:
Rep 1 Time:	Rep 2 Time:	Rep 3 Time:	Rep 4 Time:	Rep 5 Time:	
Rep 1 Score:	Rep 2 Score:	Rep 3 Score:	Rep 4 Score:	Rep 5 Score:	**Total Score:**

STAND YOUR GROUND

www.GUNFIGHTERSERIES.com ©

Date:	Location:	Weapon:	Sights:	Body / Head	Notes:
Rep 1 Time:	Rep 2 Time:	Rep 3 Time:	Rep 4 Time:	Rep 5 Time:	
Rep 1 Score:	Rep 2 Score:	Rep 3 Score:	Rep 4 Score:	Rep 5 Score:	Total Score:

Date:	Location:	Weapon:	Sights:	Body / Head	Notes:
Rep 1 Time:	Rep 2 Time:	Rep 3 Time:	Rep 4 Time:	Rep 5 Time:	
Rep 1 Score:	Rep 2 Score:	Rep 3 Score:	Rep 4 Score:	Rep 5 Score:	Total Score:

Date:	Location:	Weapon:	Sights:	Body / Head	Notes:
Rep 1 Time:	Rep 2 Time:	Rep 3 Time:	Rep 4 Time:	Rep 5 Time:	
Rep 1 Score:	Rep 2 Score:	Rep 3 Score:	Rep 4 Score:	Rep 5 Score:	Total Score:

Date:	Location:	Weapon:	Sights:	Body / Head	Notes:
Rep 1 Time:	Rep 2 Time:	Rep 3 Time:	Rep 4 Time:	Rep 5 Time:	
Rep 1 Score:	Rep 2 Score:	Rep 3 Score:	Rep 4 Score:	Rep 5 Score:	Total Score:

Date:	Location:	Weapon:	Sights:	Body / Head	Notes:
Rep 1 Time:	Rep 2 Time:	Rep 3 Time:	Rep 4 Time:	Rep 5 Time:	
Rep 1 Score:	Rep 2 Score:	Rep 3 Score:	Rep 4 Score:	Rep 5 Score:	Total Score:

STAND YOUR GROUND

Date:	Location:	Weapon:	Sights:	Body / Head	Notes:
Rep 1 Time:	Rep 2 Time:	Rep 3 Time:	Rep 4 Time:	Rep 5 Time:	
Rep 1 Score:	Rep 2 Score:	Rep 3 Score:	Rep 4 Score:	Rep 5 Score:	**Total Score:**

Date:	Location:	Weapon:	Sights:	Body / Head	Notes:
Rep 1 Time:	Rep 2 Time:	Rep 3 Time:	Rep 4 Time:	Rep 5 Time:	
Rep 1 Score:	Rep 2 Score:	Rep 3 Score:	Rep 4 Score:	Rep 5 Score:	**Total Score:**

Date:	Location:	Weapon:	Sights:	Body / Head	Notes:
Rep 1 Time:	Rep 2 Time:	Rep 3 Time:	Rep 4 Time:	Rep 5 Time:	
Rep 1 Score:	Rep 2 Score:	Rep 3 Score:	Rep 4 Score:	Rep 5 Score:	**Total Score:**

Date:	Location:	Weapon:	Sights:	Body / Head	Notes:
Rep 1 Time:	Rep 2 Time:	Rep 3 Time:	Rep 4 Time:	Rep 5 Time:	
Rep 1 Score:	Rep 2 Score:	Rep 3 Score:	Rep 4 Score:	Rep 5 Score:	**Total Score:**

Date:	Location:	Weapon:	Sights:	Body / Head	Notes:
Rep 1 Time:	Rep 2 Time:	Rep 3 Time:	Rep 4 Time:	Rep 5 Time:	
Rep 1 Score:	Rep 2 Score:	Rep 3 Score:	Rep 4 Score:	Rep 5 Score:	**Total Score:**

Fundamental Carbine ©

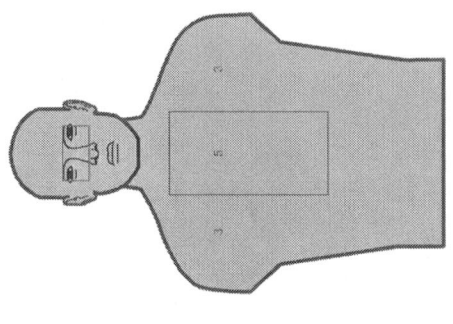

RICE PADDY

Purpose: Increase the accuracy and competency of the squatting position.

Distance: 35 Yards.

Target: JD-QUAL1

Par Time: 7 Seconds.

Extra Equipment Needed: Shot timer. Spotting scope (optional).

Rounds Fired Per Rep: 3 Rounds.   **Total Rounds Fired:** 15 Rounds.

Point Penalty: As per target score.

Repetitions: 5 Reps.

Starting Position & Condition: Standing - Any ready position you choose. Condition 1.

Description: At the timer beep, go to the squatting position while keeping the carbine pointed down range at the targets direction. Take aim at the target and fire 3 rounds into the A Zone (5 point) body or head box. Record how many times you made par time and hit within the A Zone (5 point) body or head box. Not making par time and/or not making the minimum goal points makes the drill a failure.

Goals: Novice: 45 Points within par.   Expert: 67 Points within par.   Gunfighter: 75 Points within par.

RICE PADDY

Date:	Location:	Weapon:	Sights:	Body / Head	Notes:
Rep 1 Time:	Rep 2 Time:	Rep 3 Time:	Rep 4 Time:	Rep 5 Time:	
Rep 1 Score:	Rep 2 Score:	Rep 3 Score:	Rep 4 Score:	Rep 5 Score:	**Total Score:**

Date:	Location:	Weapon:	Sights:	Body / Head	Notes:
Rep 1 Time:	Rep 2 Time:	Rep 3 Time:	Rep 4 Time:	Rep 5 Time:	
Rep 1 Score:	Rep 2 Score:	Rep 3 Score:	Rep 4 Score:	Rep 5 Score:	**Total Score:**

Date:	Location:	Weapon:	Sights:	Body / Head	Notes:
Rep 1 Time:	Rep 2 Time:	Rep 3 Time:	Rep 4 Time:	Rep 5 Time:	
Rep 1 Score:	Rep 2 Score:	Rep 3 Score:	Rep 4 Score:	Rep 5 Score:	**Total Score:**

Date:	Location:	Weapon:	Sights:	Body / Head	Notes:
Rep 1 Time:	Rep 2 Time:	Rep 3 Time:	Rep 4 Time:	Rep 5 Time:	
Rep 1 Score:	Rep 2 Score:	Rep 3 Score:	Rep 4 Score:	Rep 5 Score:	**Total Score:**

Date:	Location:	Weapon:	Sights:	Body / Head	Notes:
Rep 1 Time:	Rep 2 Time:	Rep 3 Time:	Rep 4 Time:	Rep 5 Time:	
Rep 1 Score:	Rep 2 Score:	Rep 3 Score:	Rep 4 Score:	Rep 5 Score:	**Total Score:**

STAND YOUR GROUND

Date:	Location:	Weapon:	Sights:	Body / Head	Notes:
Rep 1 Time:	Rep 2 Time:	Rep 3 Time:	Rep 4 Time:	Rep 5 Time:	
Rep 1 Score:	Rep 2 Score:	Rep 3 Score:	Rep 4 Score:	Rep 5 Score:	**Total Score:**

Date:	Location:	Weapon:	Sights:	Body / Head	Notes:
Rep 1 Time:	Rep 2 Time:	Rep 3 Time:	Rep 4 Time:	Rep 5 Time:	
Rep 1 Score:	Rep 2 Score:	Rep 3 Score:	Rep 4 Score:	Rep 5 Score:	**Total Score:**

Date:	Location:	Weapon:	Sights:	Body / Head	Notes:
Rep 1 Time:	Rep 2 Time:	Rep 3 Time:	Rep 4 Time:	Rep 5 Time:	
Rep 1 Score:	Rep 2 Score:	Rep 3 Score:	Rep 4 Score:	Rep 5 Score:	**Total Score:**

Date:	Location:	Weapon:	Sights:	Body / Head	Notes:
Rep 1 Time:	Rep 2 Time:	Rep 3 Time:	Rep 4 Time:	Rep 5 Time:	
Rep 1 Score:	Rep 2 Score:	Rep 3 Score:	Rep 4 Score:	Rep 5 Score:	**Total Score:**

Date:	Location:	Weapon:	Sights:	Body / Head	Notes:
Rep 1 Time:	Rep 2 Time:	Rep 3 Time:	Rep 4 Time:	Rep 5 Time:	
Rep 1 Score:	Rep 2 Score:	Rep 3 Score:	Rep 4 Score:	Rep 5 Score:	**Total Score:**

RICE PADDY

Date:	Location:	Weapon:	Sights:	Body / Head	Notes:
Rep 1 Time:	Rep 2 Time:	Rep 3 Time:	Rep 4 Time:	Rep 5 Time:	
Rep 1 Score:	Rep 2 Score:	Rep 3 Score:	Rep 4 Score:	Rep 5 Score:	**Total Score:**

Date:	Location:	Weapon:	Sights:	Body / Head	Notes:
Rep 1 Time:	Rep 2 Time:	Rep 3 Time:	Rep 4 Time:	Rep 5 Time:	
Rep 1 Score:	Rep 2 Score:	Rep 3 Score:	Rep 4 Score:	Rep 5 Score:	**Total Score:**

Date:	Location:	Weapon:	Sights:	Body / Head	Notes:
Rep 1 Time:	Rep 2 Time:	Rep 3 Time:	Rep 4 Time:	Rep 5 Time:	
Rep 1 Score:	Rep 2 Score:	Rep 3 Score:	Rep 4 Score:	Rep 5 Score:	**Total Score:**

Date:	Location:	Weapon:	Sights:	Body / Head	Notes:
Rep 1 Time:	Rep 2 Time:	Rep 3 Time:	Rep 4 Time:	Rep 5 Time:	
Rep 1 Score:	Rep 2 Score:	Rep 3 Score:	Rep 4 Score:	Rep 5 Score:	**Total Score:**

Date:	Location:	Weapon:	Sights:	Body / Head	Notes:
Rep 1 Time:	Rep 2 Time:	Rep 3 Time:	Rep 4 Time:	Rep 5 Time:	
Rep 1 Score:	Rep 2 Score:	Rep 3 Score:	Rep 4 Score:	Rep 5 Score:	**Total Score:**

STAND YOUR GROUND

Date:	Location:	Weapon:	Sights:	Body / Head	Notes:
Rep 1 Time:	Rep 2 Time:	Rep 3 Time:	Rep 4 Time:	Rep 5 Time:	
Rep 1 Score:	Rep 2 Score:	Rep 3 Score:	Rep 4 Score:	Rep 5 Score:	**Total Score:**

Date:	Location:	Weapon:	Sights:	Body / Head	Notes:
Rep 1 Time:	Rep 2 Time:	Rep 3 Time:	Rep 4 Time:	Rep 5 Time:	
Rep 1 Score:	Rep 2 Score:	Rep 3 Score:	Rep 4 Score:	Rep 5 Score:	**Total Score:**

Date:	Location:	Weapon:	Sights:	Body / Head	Notes:
Rep 1 Time:	Rep 2 Time:	Rep 3 Time:	Rep 4 Time:	Rep 5 Time:	
Rep 1 Score:	Rep 2 Score:	Rep 3 Score:	Rep 4 Score:	Rep 5 Score:	**Total Score:**

Date:	Location:	Weapon:	Sights:	Body / Head	Notes:
Rep 1 Time:	Rep 2 Time:	Rep 3 Time:	Rep 4 Time:	Rep 5 Time:	
Rep 1 Score:	Rep 2 Score:	Rep 3 Score:	Rep 4 Score:	Rep 5 Score:	**Total Score:**

Date:	Location:	Weapon:	Sights:	Body / Head	Notes:
Rep 1 Time:	Rep 2 Time:	Rep 3 Time:	Rep 4 Time:	Rep 5 Time:	
Rep 1 Score:	Rep 2 Score:	Rep 3 Score:	Rep 4 Score:	Rep 5 Score:	**Total Score:**

RICE PADDY

Date:	Location:	Weapon:	Sights:	Body / Head	Notes:
Rep 1 Time:	Rep 2 Time:	Rep 3 Time:	Rep 4 Time:	Rep 5 Time:	
Rep 1 Score:	Rep 2 Score:	Rep 3 Score:	Rep 4 Score:	Rep 5 Score:	**Total Score:**

Date:	Location:	Weapon:	Sights:	Body / Head	Notes:
Rep 1 Time:	Rep 2 Time:	Rep 3 Time:	Rep 4 Time:	Rep 5 Time:	
Rep 1 Score:	Rep 2 Score:	Rep 3 Score:	Rep 4 Score:	Rep 5 Score:	**Total Score:**

Date:	Location:	Weapon:	Sights:	Body / Head	Notes:
Rep 1 Time:	Rep 2 Time:	Rep 3 Time:	Rep 4 Time:	Rep 5 Time:	
Rep 1 Score:	Rep 2 Score:	Rep 3 Score:	Rep 4 Score:	Rep 5 Score:	**Total Score:**

Date:	Location:	Weapon:	Sights:	Body / Head	Notes:
Rep 1 Time:	Rep 2 Time:	Rep 3 Time:	Rep 4 Time:	Rep 5 Time:	
Rep 1 Score:	Rep 2 Score:	Rep 3 Score:	Rep 4 Score:	Rep 5 Score:	**Total Score:**

Date:	Location:	Weapon:	Sights:	Body / Head	Notes:
Rep 1 Time:	Rep 2 Time:	Rep 3 Time:	Rep 4 Time:	Rep 5 Time:	
Rep 1 Score:	Rep 2 Score:	Rep 3 Score:	Rep 4 Score:	Rep 5 Score:	**Total Score:**

Fundamental Carbine ©

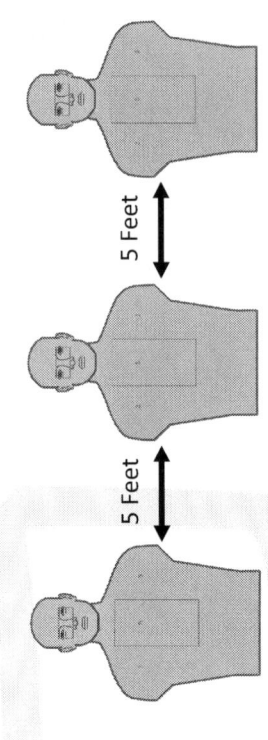

RHODIE MIKE

Purpose: Increase accuracy, speed and recoil management with multiple targets.

Distance: 15 Yards.

Target: JD-QUAL1 X 3. Targets set up 5 feet apart at 15 yards.

Par Time: 9 Seconds.

Extra Equipment Needed: Shot timer.

Rounds Fired per Rep: 9 Rounds.　　　**Total Rounds Fired:** 27 Rounds.

Point Penalty: Go / No Go.

Repetitions: 3 Reps.

Starting Position & Condition: Standing - Low ready.　Condition 1.

Description: At the timer beep, fire 2 rounds into the A Zone (5 point) body box, then 1 round to the A Zone (5 point) head box, transition to next target with the same shot pattern and then transition to the last target with the same shot pattern. Goal is all rounds with goal par time and within A Zone boxes. If you fail goal par time or have rounds out of designated A Zone (5 point) boxes during a repetition, the drill repetition is a failure. The more accomplished shooter you become, the faster you will at this drill.

Goals: Novice: 9 Seconds.　　　Expert: 8 Seconds.　　　Gunfighter: 6 Seconds.

RHODIE MIKE

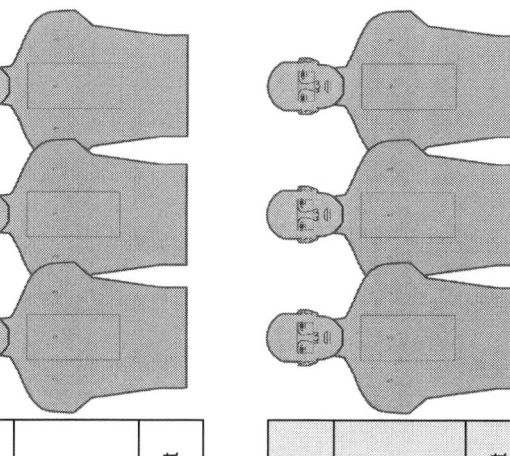
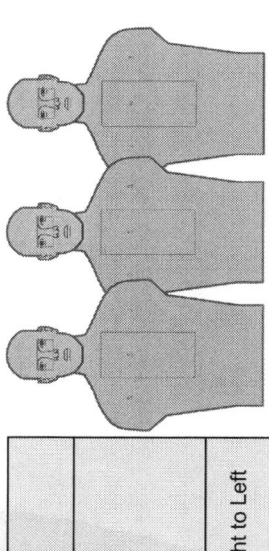
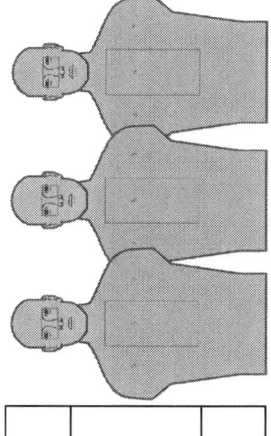

Date:	Location:	Weapon:	Sights:
Rep 1 Time:	**Rep 2 Time:**	**Rep 3 Time:**	Notes:
# Outside A Box:	# Outside A Box:	# Outside A Box:	
Rep 1: Go / No Go	Rep 2: Go / No Go	Rep 3: Go / No Go	Left to Right / Right to Left

Date:	Location:	Weapon:	Sights:
Rep 1 Time:	**Rep 2 Time:**	**Rep 3 Time:**	Notes:
# Outside A Box:	# Outside A Box:	# Outside A Box:	
Rep 1: Go / No Go	Rep 2: Go / No Go	Rep 3: Go / No Go	Left to Right / Right to Left

Date:	Location:	Weapon:	Sights:
Rep 1 Time:	**Rep 2 Time:**	**Rep 3 Time:**	Notes:
# Outside A Box:	# Outside A Box:	# Outside A Box:	
Rep 1: Go / No Go	Rep 2: Go / No Go	Rep 3: Go / No Go	Left to Right / Right to Left

Multiple Target Drills - 1

Fundamental Carbine ©

RHODIE MIKE

www.GUNFIGHTERSERIES.com ©

Date:	Location:	Weapon:	Sights:
Rep 1 Time:	**Rep 2 Time:**	**Rep 3 Time:**	Notes:
# Outside A Box:	# Outside A Box:	# Outside A Box:	
Rep 1: Go / No Go	Rep 2: Go / No Go	Rep 3: Go / No Go	Left to Right / Right to Left

Date:	Location:	Weapon:	Sights:
Rep 1 Time:	**Rep 2 Time:**	**Rep 3 Time:**	Notes:
# Outside A Box:	# Outside A Box:	# Outside A Box:	
Rep 1: Go / No Go	Rep 2: Go / No Go	Rep 3: Go / No Go	Left to Right / Right to Left

Date:	Location:	Weapon:	Sights:
Rep 1 Time:	**Rep 2 Time:**	**Rep 3 Time:**	Notes:
# Outside A Box:	# Outside A Box:	# Outside A Box:	
Rep 1: Go / No Go	Rep 2: Go / No Go	Rep 3: Go / No Go	Left to Right / Right to Left

RHODIE MIKE

Date:	Location:	Weapon:	Sights:
Rep 1 Time:	**Rep 2 Time:**	**Rep 3 Time:**	Notes:
# Outside A Box:	# Outside A Box:	# Outside A Box:	
Rep 1: Go / No Go	Rep 2: Go / No Go	Rep 3: Go / No Go	Left to Right / Right to Left

Date:	Location:	Weapon:	Sights:
Rep 1 Time:	**Rep 2 Time:**	**Rep 3 Time:**	Notes:
# Outside A Box:	# Outside A Box:	# Outside A Box:	
Rep 1: Go / No Go	Rep 2: Go / No Go	Rep 3: Go / No Go	Left to Right / Right to Left

Date:	Location:	Weapon:	Sights:
Rep 1 Time:	**Rep 2 Time:**	**Rep 3 Time:**	Notes:
# Outside A Box:	# Outside A Box:	# Outside A Box:	
Rep 1: Go / No Go	Rep 2: Go / No Go	Rep 3: Go / No Go	Left to Right / Right to Left

Multiple Target Drills - 1

Fundamental Carbine ©

RHODIE MIKE

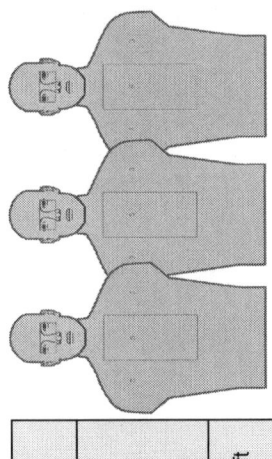
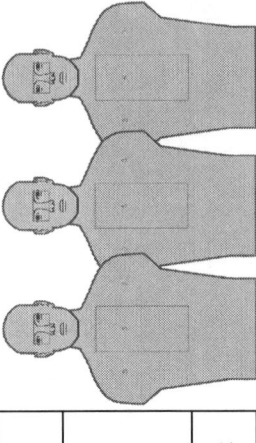

Date:	Location:	Weapon:	Sights:
Rep 1 Time:	**Rep 2 Time:**	**Rep 3 Time:**	Notes:
# Outside A Box:	# Outside A Box:	# Outside A Box:	
Rep 1: Go / No Go	Rep 2: Go / No Go	Rep 3: Go / No Go	Left to Right / Right to Left

Date:	Location:	Weapon:	Sights:
Rep 1 Time:	**Rep 2 Time:**	**Rep 3 Time:**	Notes:
# Outside A Box:	# Outside A Box:	# Outside A Box:	
Rep 1: Go / No Go	Rep 2: Go / No Go	Rep 3: Go / No Go	Left to Right / Right to Left

Date:	Location:	Weapon:	Sights:
Rep 1 Time:	**Rep 2 Time:**	**Rep 3 Time:**	Notes:
# Outside A Box:	# Outside A Box:	# Outside A Box:	
Rep 1: Go / No Go	Rep 2: Go / No Go	Rep 3: Go / No Go	Left to Right / Right to Left

RHODIE MIKE

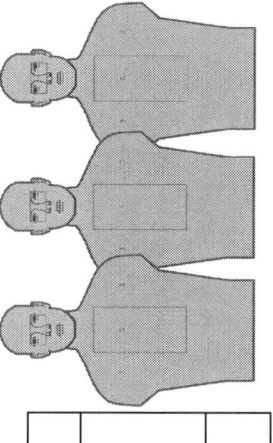
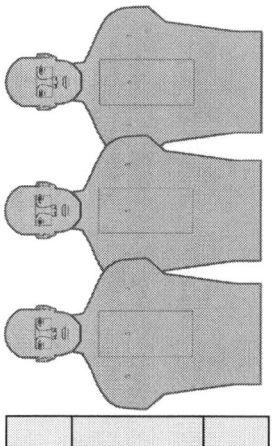
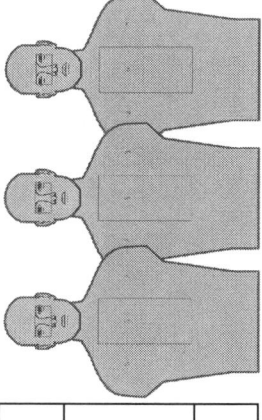

Date:	Location:	Weapon:	Sights:
Rep 1 Time:	**Rep 2 Time:**	**Rep 3 Time:**	Notes:
# Outside A Box:	# Outside A Box:	# Outside A Box:	
Rep 1: Go / No Go	Rep 2: Go / No Go	Rep 3: Go / No Go	Left to Right / Right to Left

Date:	Location:	Weapon:	Sights:
Rep 1 Time:	**Rep 2 Time:**	**Rep 3 Time:**	Notes:
# Outside A Box:	# Outside A Box:	# Outside A Box:	
Rep 1: Go / No Go	Rep 2: Go / No Go	Rep 3: Go / No Go	Left to Right / Right to Left

Date:	Location:	Weapon:	Sights:
Rep 1 Time:	**Rep 2 Time:**	**Rep 3 Time:**	Notes:
# Outside A Box:	# Outside A Box:	# Outside A Box:	
Rep 1: Go / No Go	Rep 2: Go / No Go	Rep 3: Go / No Go	Left to Right / Right to Left

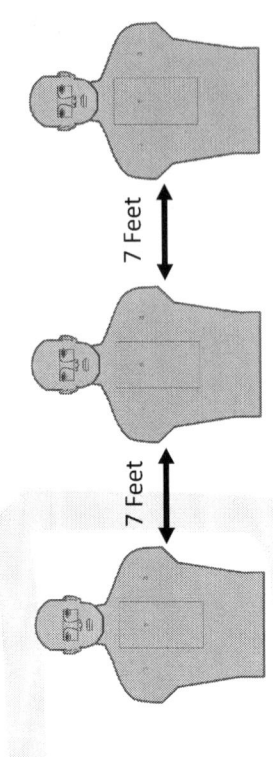

RAKE'M

Purpose: Increase dexterity with carbine while engaging multiple targets.

Distance: 10 Yards.

Target: JD-QUAL1 X 3. Targets set up 7 feet apart at 10 yards.

Par Time: 15 Seconds.

Extra Equipment Needed: Shot timer.

Total Rounds Fired: 18 Rounds.

Point Penalty: As per target score.

Starting Position & Condition: Standing - High ready. Condition 1.

Description: At the timer beep, fire 1 round into the A Zone (5 point) body box of each target. Then fire 2 more rounds into the A Zone (5 point) body box of the last target engaged and move back through targets firing 2 rounds into each A Zone (5 point) body box. Once 2 rounds have been fired through all targets; fire 3 more rounds into the A Zone (5 point) body box of the last target engaged and move back through targets firing 3 rounds into each A Zone (5 point) body box. Each target should have 6 rounds each in the A Zone (5 point) body box at the end of the drill. For every hit in the 3 scoring zone add 2 seconds to your time. For every hit in the 0 scoring zone add 5 seconds to your time.

Goals: Novice: 15+ Seconds.   Expert: 6.5 Seconds.   Gunfighter: 5 Seconds.

RAKE'M

Date:	Location:	Weapon:	Sights:
Body / Head	Time:	+ Penalties:	= Score:
Notes:			

Date:	Location:	Weapon:	Sights:
Body / Head	Time:	+ Penalties:	= Score:
Notes:			

Date:	Location:	Weapon:	Sights:
Body / Head	Time:	+ Penalties:	= Score:
Notes:			

Date:	Location:	Weapon:	Sights:
Body / Head	Time:	+ Penalties:	= Score:
Notes:			

Multiple Target Drills - 2

Fundamental Carbine ©

RAKE'M

www.GUNFIGHTERSERIES.com ©

Date:	Location:	Weapon:	Sights:
Body / Head	Time:	+ Penalties:	= **Score:**
Notes:			

Date:	Location:	Weapon:	Sights:
Body / Head	Time:	+ Penalties:	= **Score:**
Notes:			

Date:	Location:	Weapon:	Sights:
Body / Head	Time:	+ Penalties:	= **Score:**
Notes:			

Date:	Location:	Weapon:	Sights:
Body / Head	Time:	+ Penalties:	= **Score:**
Notes:			

RAKE'M

Date:	Location:	Weapon:	Sights:
Body / Head	Time:	+ Penalties:	= **Score:**

Notes:

Date:	Location:	Weapon:	Sights:
Body / Head	Time:	+ Penalties:	= **Score:**

Notes:

Date:	Location:	Weapon:	Sights:
Body / Head	Time:	+ Penalties:	= **Score:**

Notes:

Date:	Location:	Weapon:	Sights:
Body / Head	Time:	+ Penalties:	= **Score:**

Notes:

Fundamental Carbine ©

Multiple Target Drills - 2

RAKE'M

www.GUNFIGHTERSERIES.com ©

Date:	Location:	Weapon:	Sights:
Body / Head	Time:	+ Penalties:	= Score:
Notes:			

Date:	Location:	Weapon:	Sights:
Body / Head	Time:	+ Penalties:	= Score:
Notes:			

Date:	Location:	Weapon:	Sights:
Body / Head	Time:	+ Penalties:	= Score:
Notes:			

Date:	Location:	Weapon:	Sights:
Body / Head	Time:	+ Penalties:	= Score:
Notes:			

RAKE'M

Date:	Location:	Weapon:	Sights:
Body / Head	Time:	+ Penalties:	= Score:
Notes:			

Date:	Location:	Weapon:	Sights:
Body / Head	Time:	+ Penalties:	= Score:
Notes:			

Date:	Location:	Weapon:	Sights:
Body / Head	Time:	+ Penalties:	= Score:
Notes:			

Date:	Location:	Weapon:	Sights:
Body / Head	Time:	+ Penalties:	= Score:
Notes:			

Multiple Target Drills - 2

Fundamental Carbine ©

REALITY HITS THE FAN

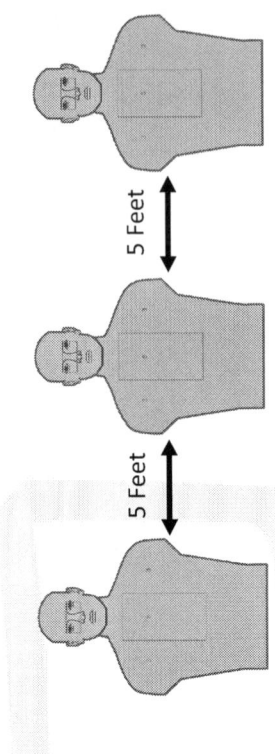

Purpose: Engaging multiple targets while under stress.

Distance: 25 Yards.

Target: JD-QUAL1 X 3. Place 3 targets 5 feet apart at 25 yards.

Extra Equipment Needed: Shot timer, 2 magazines, 1 magazine pouch.

Rounds Fired per Rep: 9 Rounds.   **Total Rounds Fired:** 27 Rounds.

Point Penalty: As per target score.

Repetitions: 3 Reps.

Starting Position & Condition: Standing - High ready. Condition 3 with hammer cocked.

Description: Have 1 magazine with 3 rounds inserted in the weapon and another magazine full at start of drill. At the timer beep, attempt to fire, hearing the click, perform a type 1 malfunction clearance. Upon clearing weapon, fire 3 rounds into the A Zone (5 point) body box of each target. You will have to perform an emergency reload during drill. Record time and score targets for each repetition. For every hit in the 3 scoring zone add 2 seconds to your time. For every hit in the 0 scoring zone add 5 seconds to your time. Add the penalty time onto your recorded time for that repetition. Average all of the repetitions and there is your time. The more accurate and smooth you become, the more your time will come down.

Variations: Stress multiplier - Add a 50 yard run before drill, shoot on support side and starting with a magazine with any number of rounds that will still force you to do a reload at some point during drill.

REALITY HITS THE FAN

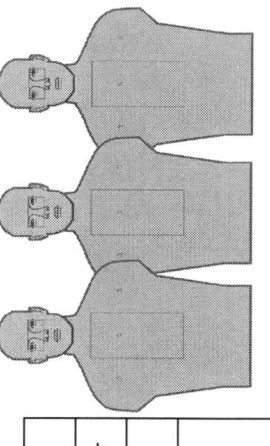
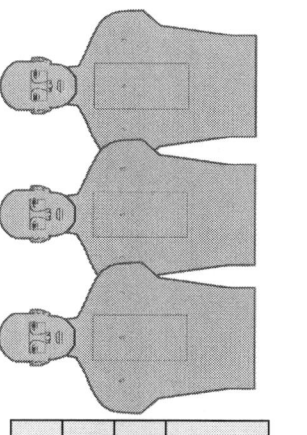
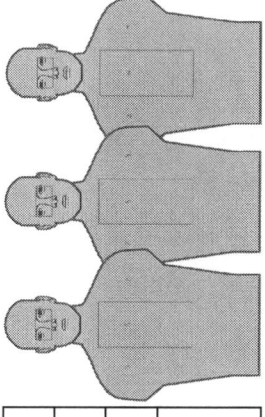

Date:	Location:	Weapon:	Sights:
Rep 1 1st Shot:	Rep 2 1st Shot:	Rep 3 1st Shot:	Standard / Stress Multiplier
Rep 1 Time:	Rep 2 Time:	Rep 3 Time:	Left to Right / Right to Left
+ Penalties:	+ Penalties:	+ Penalties:	Notes:
Rep 1 Score:	**Rep 2 Score:**	**Rep 3 Score:**	

Date:	Location:	Weapon:	Sights:
Rep 1 1st Shot:	Rep 2 1st Shot:	Rep 3 1st Shot:	Standard / Stress Multiplier
Rep 1 Time:	Rep 2 Time:	Rep 3 Time:	Left to Right / Right to Left
+ Penalties:	+ Penalties:	+ Penalties:	Notes:
Rep 1 Score:	**Rep 2 Score:**	**Rep 3 Score:**	

Date:	Location:	Weapon:	Sights:
Rep 1 1st Shot:	Rep 2 1st Shot:	Rep 3 1st Shot:	Standard / Stress Multiplier
Rep 1 Time:	Rep 2 Time:	Rep 3 Time:	Left to Right / Right to Left
+ Penalties:	+ Penalties:	+ Penalties:	Notes:
Rep 1 Score:	**Rep 2 Score:**	**Rep 3 Score:**	

Multiple Target Drills - 3

REALITY HITS THE FAN

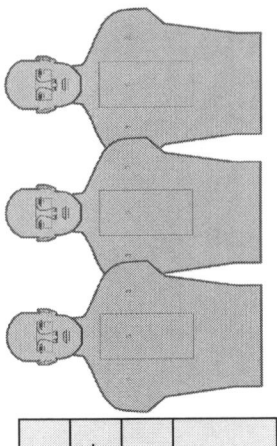
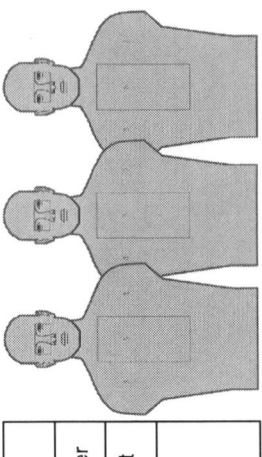

Date:	Location:	Weapon:	Sights:
Rep 1 1st Shot:	Rep 2 1st Shot:	Rep 3 1st Shot:	Standard / Stress Multiplier
Rep 1 Time:	Rep 2 Time:	Rep 3 Time:	Left to Right / Right to Left
+ Penalties:	+ Penalties:	+ Penalties:	Notes:
Rep 1 Score:	**Rep 2 Score:**	**Rep 3 Score:**	

Date:	Location:	Weapon:	Sights:
Rep 1 1st Shot:	Rep 2 1st Shot:	Rep 3 1st Shot:	Standard / Stress Multiplier
Rep 1 Time:	Rep 2 Time:	Rep 3 Time:	Left to Right / Right to Left
+ Penalties:	+ Penalties:	+ Penalties:	Notes:
Rep 1 Score:	**Rep 2 Score:**	**Rep 3 Score:**	

Date:	Location:	Weapon:	Sights:
Rep 1 1st Shot:	Rep 2 1st Shot:	Rep 3 1st Shot:	Standard / Stress Multiplier
Rep 1 Time:	Rep 2 Time:	Rep 3 Time:	Left to Right / Right to Left
+ Penalties:	+ Penalties:	+ Penalties:	Notes:
Rep 1 Score:	**Rep 2 Score:**	**Rep 3 Score:**	

REALITY HITS THE FAN

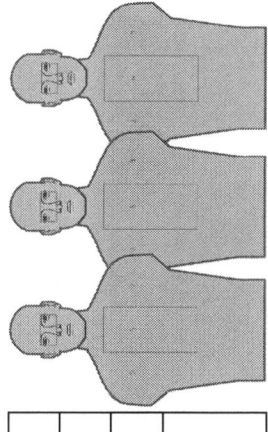

Date:	Location:	Weapon:	Sights:
Rep 1 1st Shot:	Rep 2 1st Shot:	Rep 3 1st Shot:	Standard / Stress Multiplier
Rep 1 Time:	Rep 2 Time:	Rep 3 Time:	Left to Right / Right to Left
+ Penalties:	+ Penalties:	+ Penalties:	Notes:
Rep 1 Score:	**Rep 2 Score:**	**Rep 3 Score:**	

Date:	Location:	Weapon:	Sights:
Rep 1 1st Shot:	Rep 2 1st Shot:	Rep 3 1st Shot:	Standard / Stress Multiplier
Rep 1 Time:	Rep 2 Time:	Rep 3 Time:	Left to Right / Right to Left
+ Penalties:	+ Penalties:	+ Penalties:	Notes:
Rep 1 Score:	**Rep 2 Score:**	**Rep 3 Score:**	

Date:	Location:	Weapon:	Sights:
Rep 1 1st Shot:	Rep 2 1st Shot:	Rep 3 1st Shot:	Standard / Stress Multiplier
Rep 1 Time:	Rep 2 Time:	Rep 3 Time:	Left to Right / Right to Left
+ Penalties:	+ Penalties:	+ Penalties:	Notes:
Rep 1 Score:	**Rep 2 Score:**	**Rep 3 Score:**	

REALITY HITS THE FAN

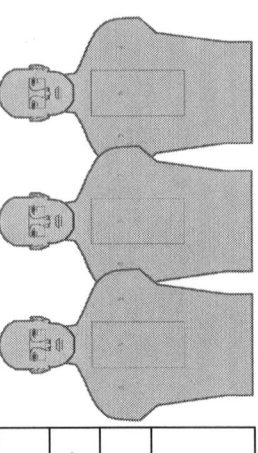

www.GUNFIGHTERSERIES.com ©

Date:	Location:	Weapon:	Sights:
Rep 1 1st Shot:	Rep 2 1st Shot:	Rep 3 1st Shot:	Standard / Stress Multiplier
Rep 1 Time:	Rep 2 Time:	Rep 3 Time:	Left to Right / Right to Left
+ Penalties:	+ Penalties:	+ Penalties:	Notes:
Rep 1 Score:	**Rep 2 Score:**	**Rep 3 Score:**	

Date:	Location:	Weapon:	Sights:
Rep 1 1st Shot:	Rep 2 1st Shot:	Rep 3 1st Shot:	Standard / Stress Multiplier
Rep 1 Time:	Rep 2 Time:	Rep 3 Time:	Left to Right / Right to Left
+ Penalties:	+ Penalties:	+ Penalties:	Notes:
Rep 1 Score:	**Rep 2 Score:**	**Rep 3 Score:**	

Date:	Location:	Weapon:	Sights:
Rep 1 1st Shot:	Rep 2 1st Shot:	Rep 3 1st Shot:	Standard / Stress Multiplier
Rep 1 Time:	Rep 2 Time:	Rep 3 Time:	Left to Right / Right to Left
+ Penalties:	+ Penalties:	+ Penalties:	Notes:
Rep 1 Score:	**Rep 2 Score:**	**Rep 3 Score:**	

REALITY HITS THE FAN

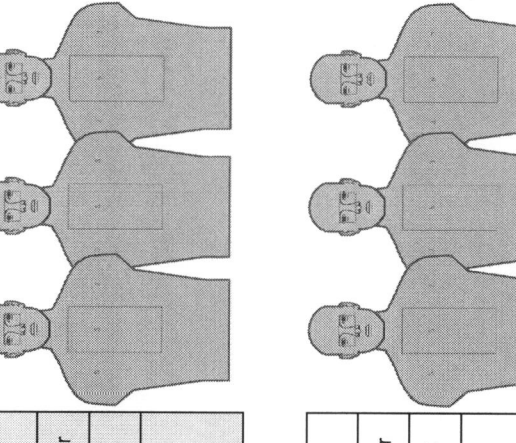

Date:	Location:	Weapon:	Sights:
Rep 1 1st Shot:	Rep 2 1st Shot:	Rep 3 1st Shot:	Standard / Stress Multiplier
Rep 1 Time:	Rep 2 Time:	Rep 3 Time:	Left to Right / Right to Left
+ Penalties:	+ Penalties:	+ Penalties:	Notes:
Rep 1 Score:	**Rep 2 Score:**	**Rep 3 Score:**	

Date:	Location:	Weapon:	Sights:
Rep 1 1st Shot:	Rep 2 1st Shot:	Rep 3 1st Shot:	Standard / Stress Multiplier
Rep 1 Time:	Rep 2 Time:	Rep 3 Time:	Left to Right / Right to Left
+ Penalties:	+ Penalties:	+ Penalties:	Notes:
Rep 1 Score:	**Rep 2 Score:**	**Rep 3 Score:**	

Date:	Location:	Weapon:	Sights:
Rep 1 1st Shot:	Rep 2 1st Shot:	Rep 3 1st Shot:	Standard / Stress Multiplier
Rep 1 Time:	Rep 2 Time:	Rep 3 Time:	Left to Right / Right to Left
+ Penalties:	+ Penalties:	+ Penalties:	Notes:
Rep 1 Score:	**Rep 2 Score:**	**Rep 3 Score:**	

Multiple Target Drills - 3

Fundamental Carbine ©

SPEEDY

Purpose: Engaging multiple targets at close quarters.

Distance: 7 Yards.

Target: JD-QUAL1 X 3. Place 3 targets 5 feet apart at 7 yards.

Extra Equipment Needed: Shot timer.

Rounds Fired per Rep: 15 Rounds. **Total Rounds Fired:** 30 Rounds.

Point Penalty: As per target score.

Repetitions: 2 Reps.

Starting Position & Condition: Standing - Low ready. Condition 1.

Description: At the timer beep, fire 5 rounds into the A Zone (5 point) body box of each target. For every hit in the 0 scoring zone add 5 seconds to your time.

Goals: Novice: 10 Seconds.   Expert: 5 Seconds.   Gunfighter: 4 Seconds.

Note: Fastest time ever witnessed is 2.89 seconds!

Variations: Stress multiplier – Add a 50 yard run before drill, shoot on non-dominate side and/or add distance.

SPEEDY

Date:	Weapon:	Sights:	Standard / Stress Multiplier
Rep 1 Time:	+ Penalties:	= **Score:**	Notes:
Rep 2 Time:	+ Penalties:	= **Score:**	

Date:	Weapon:	Sights:	Standard / Stress Multiplier
Rep 1 Time:	+ Penalties:	= **Score:**	Notes:
Rep 2 Time:	+ Penalties:	= **Score:**	

Date:	Weapon:	Sights:	Standard / Stress Multiplier
Rep 1 Time:	+ Penalties:	= **Score:**	Notes:
Rep 2 Time:	+ Penalties:	= **Score:**	

Date:	Weapon:	Sights:	Standard / Stress Multiplier
Rep 1 Time:	+ Penalties:	= **Score:**	Notes:
Rep 2 Time:	+ Penalties:	= **Score:**	

SPEEDY

www.GUNFIGHTERSERIES.com ©

Date:	Weapon:	Sights:	Standard / Stress Multiplier
Rep 1 Time:	+ Penalties:	= Score:	Notes:
Rep 2 Time:	+ Penalties:	= Score:	

Date:	Weapon:	Sights:	Standard / Stress Multiplier
Rep 1 Time:	+ Penalties:	= Score:	Notes:
Rep 2 Time:	+ Penalties:	= Score:	

Date:	Weapon:	Sights:	Standard / Stress Multiplier
Rep 1 Time:	+ Penalties:	= Score:	Notes:
Rep 2 Time:	+ Penalties:	= Score:	

Date:	Weapon:	Sights:	Standard / Stress Multiplier
Rep 1 Time:	+ Penalties:	= Score:	Notes:
Rep 2 Time:	+ Penalties:	= Score:	

SPEEDY

Date:	Weapon:	Sights:	Standard / Stress Multiplier
Rep 1 Time:	+ Penalties:	= Score:	Notes:
Rep 2 Time:	+ Penalties:	= Score:	

Date:	Weapon:	Sights:	Standard / Stress Multiplier
Rep 1 Time:	+ Penalties:	= Score:	Notes:
Rep 2 Time:	+ Penalties:	= Score:	

Date:	Weapon:	Sights:	Standard / Stress Multiplier
Rep 1 Time:	+ Penalties:	= Score:	Notes:
Rep 2 Time:	+ Penalties:	= Score:	

Date:	Weapon:	Sights:	Standard / Stress Multiplier
Rep 1 Time:	+ Penalties:	= Score:	Notes:
Rep 2 Time:	+ Penalties:	= Score:	

Multiple Target Drills - 4

Fundamental Carbine ©

SPEEDY

www.GUNFIGHTERSERIES.com ©

Date:	Weapon:	Sights:	Standard / Stress Multiplier
Rep 1 Time:	+ Penalties:	= Score:	Notes:
Rep 2 Time:	+ Penalties:	= Score:	

Date:	Weapon:	Sights:	Standard / Stress Multiplier
Rep 1 Time:	+ Penalties:	= Score:	Notes:
Rep 2 Time:	+ Penalties:	= Score:	

Date:	Weapon:	Sights:	Standard / Stress Multiplier
Rep 1 Time:	+ Penalties:	= Score:	Notes:
Rep 2 Time:	+ Penalties:	= Score:	

Date:	Weapon:	Sights:	Standard / Stress Multiplier
Rep 1 Time:	+ Penalties:	= Score:	Notes:
Rep 2 Time:	+ Penalties:	= Score:	

SPEEDY

Date:	Weapon:	Sights:	Standard / Stress Multiplier
Rep 1 Time:	+ Penalties:	= Score:	Notes:
Rep 2 Time:	+ Penalties:	= Score:	

Date:	Weapon:	Sights:	Standard / Stress Multiplier
Rep 1 Time:	+ Penalties:	= Score:	Notes:
Rep 2 Time:	+ Penalties:	= Score:	

Date:	Weapon:	Sights:	Standard / Stress Multiplier
Rep 1 Time:	+ Penalties:	= Score:	Notes:
Rep 2 Time:	+ Penalties:	= Score:	

Date:	Weapon:	Sights:	Standard / Stress Multiplier
Rep 1 Time:	+ Penalties:	= Score:	Notes:
Rep 2 Time:	+ Penalties:	= Score:	

Multiple Target Drills - 4

Fundamental Carbine ©

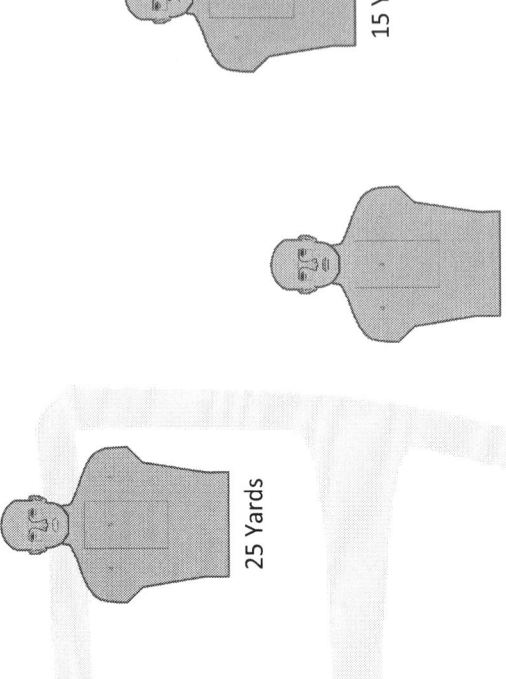

GANG LAND

Purpose: Increase discerning multiple target arrays and transitioning to pistol.

Distance: 7, 15 and 25 Yards.

Target: JD-QUAL1 X 3. Positioning of the targets laterally is up to shooter.

Par Time: 15 Seconds.

Extra Equipment Needed: Shot timer, pistol, pistol holster, carbine sling.

Rounds Fired Per Rep: 10 Rifle rounds & 5 pistol rounds.

Total Rounds Fired: 30 Rifle rounds & 15 pistol rounds.

Point Penalty: As per target score.

Repetitions: 3 Reps

Starting Position & Condition: Standing – Carbine high ready. Condition 1 with a magazine with 10 rounds inserted in the carbine.

Description: With targets placed 7, 15 and 25 yards away in any configuration. At the timer beep, fire 5 rounds per target with carbine, 5 rounds in last target with pistol. Closest target first, middle target second, farthest target last. When carbine goes dry, transition to pistol. Record time, score targets. For every hit in the 3 scoring zone, add 2 seconds to your time. For every hit in the 0 scoring zone, add 5 seconds to your time. Add the penalty time onto your recorded time for that repetition. Average all of the repetitions and there is your time. The more accurate you become, the more your time will come down.

Variations: Post pictures of a knife, pistol and club on targets with them set at different distances, engaging the most dangerous target first, second dangerous second and then the last target.

GANG LAND

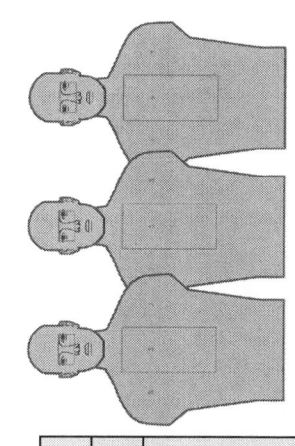
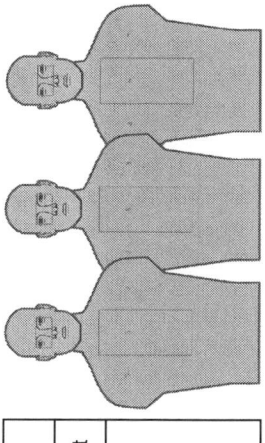

Date:	Location:	Weapon:	Sights:
Rep 1 Time:	Rep 2 Time:	Rep 3 Time:	Near to Far / Threat Assessment
+ Penalties:	+ Penalties:	+ Penalties:	
Rep 1 Score:	Rep 2 Score:	Rep 3 Score:	Notes:
Par: Go / No Go	**Par: Go / No Go**	**Par: Go / No Go**	

Date:	Location:	Weapon:	Sights:
Rep 1 Time:	Rep 2 Time:	Rep 3 Time:	Near to Far / Threat Assessment
+ Penalties:	+ Penalties:	+ Penalties:	
Rep 1 Score:	Rep 2 Score:	Rep 3 Score:	Notes:
Par: Go / No Go	**Par: Go / No Go**	**Par: Go / No Go**	

Date:	Location:	Weapon:	Sights:
Rep 1 Time:	Rep 2 Time:	Rep 3 Time:	Near to Far / Threat Assessment
+ Penalties:	+ Penalties:	+ Penalties:	
Rep 1 Score:	Rep 2 Score:	Rep 3 Score:	Notes:
Par: Go / No Go	**Par: Go / No Go**	**Par: Go / No Go**	

GANG LAND

www.GUNFIGHTERSERIES.com ©

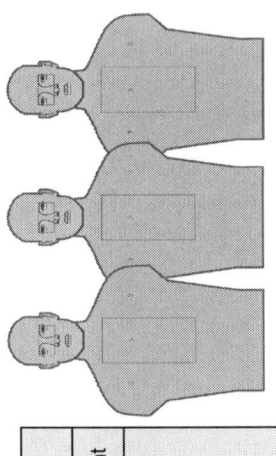
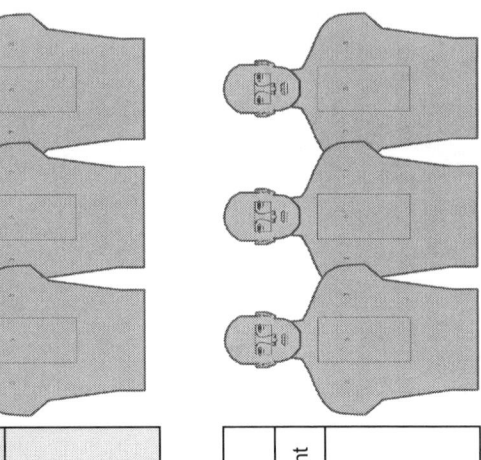

Date:	Location:	Weapon:	Sights:
Rep 1 Time:	Rep 2 Time:	Rep 3 Time:	Near to Far / Threat Assessment
+ Penalties:	+ Penalties:	+ Penalties:	Notes:
Rep 1 Score:	Rep 2 Score:	Rep 3 Score:	
Par: Go / No Go	**Par: Go / No Go**	**Par: Go / No Go**	

Date:	Location:	Weapon:	Sights:
Rep 1 Time:	Rep 2 Time:	Rep 3 Time:	Near to Far / Threat Assessment
+ Penalties:	+ Penalties:	+ Penalties:	Notes:
Rep 1 Score:	Rep 2 Score:	Rep 3 Score:	
Par: Go / No Go	**Par: Go / No Go**	**Par: Go / No Go**	

Date:	Location:	Weapon:	Sights:
Rep 1 Time:	Rep 2 Time:	Rep 3 Time:	Near to Far / Threat Assessment
+ Penalties:	+ Penalties:	+ Penalties:	Notes:
Rep 1 Score:	Rep 2 Score:	Rep 3 Score:	
Par: Go / No Go	**Par: Go / No Go**	**Par: Go / No Go**	

GANG LAND

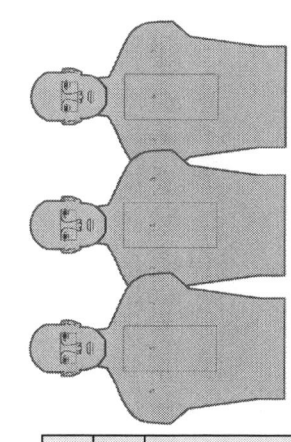
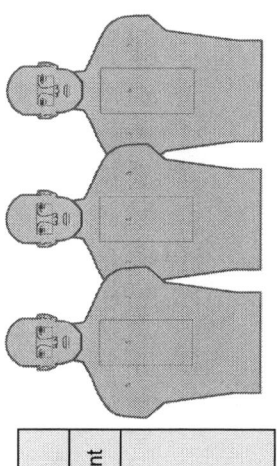
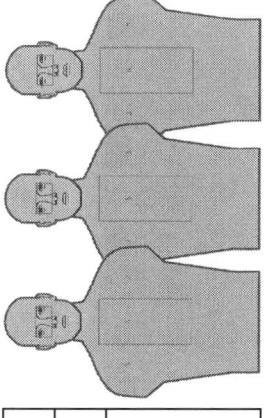

Date:	Location:	Weapon:	Sights:
Rep 1 Time:	Rep 2 Time:	Rep 3 Time:	Near to Far / Threat Assessment
+ Penalties:	+ Penalties:	+ Penalties:	Notes:
Rep 1 Score:	Rep 2 Score:	Rep 3 Score:	
Par: Go / No Go	**Par: Go / No Go**	**Par: Go / No Go**	

Date:	Location:	Weapon:	Sights:
Rep 1 Time:	Rep 2 Time:	Rep 3 Time:	Near to Far / Threat Assessment
+ Penalties:	+ Penalties:	+ Penalties:	Notes:
Rep 1 Score:	Rep 2 Score:	Rep 3 Score:	
Par: Go / No Go	**Par: Go / No Go**	**Par: Go / No Go**	

Date:	Location:	Weapon:	Sights:
Rep 1 Time:	Rep 2 Time:	Rep 3 Time:	Near to Far / Threat Assessment
+ Penalties:	+ Penalties:	+ Penalties:	Notes:
Rep 1 Score:	Rep 2 Score:	Rep 3 Score:	
Par: Go / No Go	**Par: Go / No Go**	**Par: Go / No Go**	

Fundamental Carbine © Gunfighting Skills - 1

GANG LAND

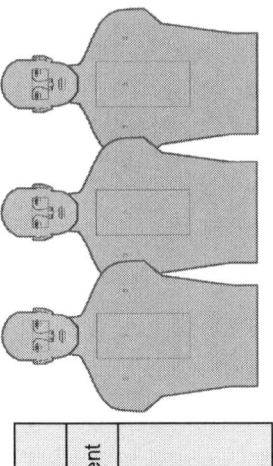
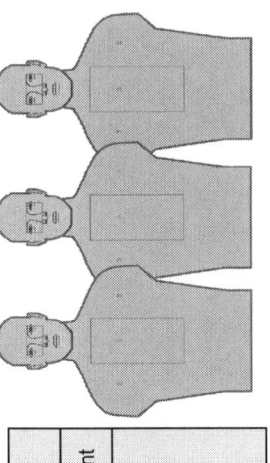
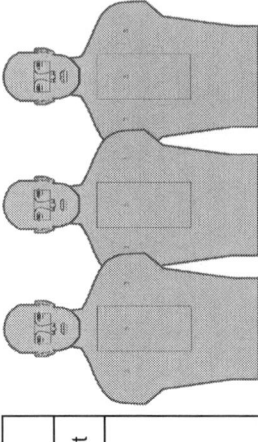

Date:	Location:	Weapon:	Sights:
Rep 1 Time:	Rep 2 Time:	Rep 3 Time:	Near to Far / Threat Assessment
+ Penalties:	+ Penalties:	+ Penalties:	Notes:
Rep 1 Score:	Rep 2 Score:	Rep 3 Score:	
Par: Go / No Go	**Par: Go / No Go**	**Par: Go / No Go**	

Date:	Location:	Weapon:	Sights:
Rep 1 Time:	Rep 2 Time:	Rep 3 Time:	Near to Far / Threat Assessment
+ Penalties:	+ Penalties:	+ Penalties:	Notes:
Rep 1 Score:	Rep 2 Score:	Rep 3 Score:	
Par: Go / No Go	**Par: Go / No Go**	**Par: Go / No Go**	

Date:	Location:	Weapon:	Sights:
Rep 1 Time:	Rep 2 Time:	Rep 3 Time:	Near to Far / Threat Assessment
+ Penalties:	+ Penalties:	+ Penalties:	Notes:
Rep 1 Score:	Rep 2 Score:	Rep 3 Score:	
Par: Go / No Go	**Par: Go / No Go**	**Par: Go / No Go**	

GANG LAND

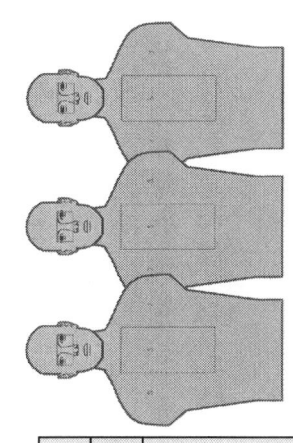

Date:	Location:	Weapon:	Sights:
Rep 1 Time:	Rep 2 Time:	Rep 3 Time:	Near to Far / Threat Assessment
+ Penalties:	+ Penalties:	+ Penalties:	Notes:
Rep 1 Score:	Rep 2 Score:	Rep 3 Score:	
Par: Go / No Go	**Par: Go / No Go**	**Par: Go / No Go**	

Date:	Location:	Weapon:	Sights:
Rep 1 Time:	Rep 2 Time:	Rep 3 Time:	Near to Far / Threat Assessment
+ Penalties:	+ Penalties:	+ Penalties:	Notes:
Rep 1 Score:	Rep 2 Score:	Rep 3 Score:	
Par: Go / No Go	**Par: Go / No Go**	**Par: Go / No Go**	

Date:	Location:	Weapon:	Sights:
Rep 1 Time:	Rep 2 Time:	Rep 3 Time:	Near to Far / Threat Assessment
+ Penalties:	+ Penalties:	+ Penalties:	Notes:
Rep 1 Score:	Rep 2 Score:	Rep 3 Score:	
Par: Go / No Go	**Par: Go / No Go**	**Par: Go / No Go**	

IN THE LINE OF FIRE

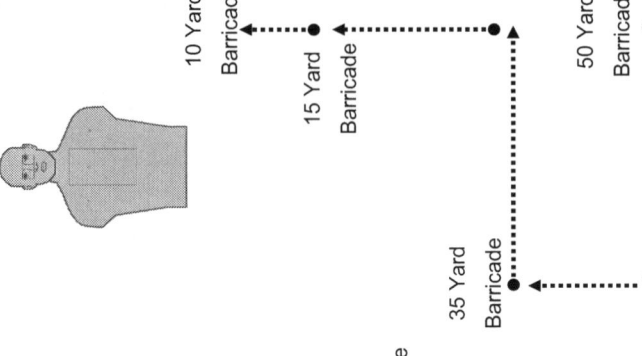

Purpose: Increase ability to get out of the line of fire and attack when using a weapon for defense.

Distance: 50, 35, 15 and 10 Yards.

Target: JD-QUAL1

Par Time: 40 Seconds.

Extra Equipment Needed: Shot timer, 4 barriers or place markers. Barriers / place markers at 10, 15, 35 and 50 yards from the target with each barrier / place maker 10 yards laterally from the previous one.

Rounds Fired per Rep: 15 Rifle rounds & 5 pistol rounds.   **Total Rounds Fired:** 45 Rifle rounds & 15 pistol rounds.

Point Penalty: Go / No Go.

Repetitions: 3 Reps.

Starting Position & Condition: Standing – Carbine port ready. Condition 1.

Description: At the timer beep, fire 5 rounds per target while moving in L shaped movements to the next closest barrier/place maker in order to limit exposure time to bad guys shooting at you. Record time, score targets. For every hit in the 3 scoring zone add 2 seconds to your time. For every hit in the 0 scoring zone add 5 seconds to your time. Not making par time, with penalty points added, is a No Go of the drill.

Variations: Stress multiplier - Immediately before the start of the drill, run 50 yards or do 2X25 yard shuttle runs, do 8 push-ups or 8 jumping jacks to get your heart rate up.

IN THE LINE OF FIRE

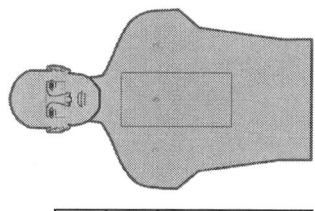

Date:	Location:	Weapon:	Sights:
			Standard / Stress Multiplier
Rep 1 Time:	Rep 2 Time:	Rep 3 Time:	
+ Penalties:	+ Penalties:	+ Penalties:	Notes:
Rep 1 Score:	Rep 2 Score:	Rep 3 Score:	
Par: Go / No Go	**Par: Go / No Go**	**Par: Go / No Go**	

Date:	Location:	Weapon:	Sights:
			Standard / Stress Multiplier
Rep 1 Time:	Rep 2 Time:	Rep 3 Time:	
+ Penalties:	+ Penalties:	+ Penalties:	Notes:
Rep 1 Score:	Rep 2 Score:	Rep 3 Score:	
Par: Go / No Go	**Par: Go / No Go**	**Par: Go / No Go**	

Date:	Location:	Weapon:	Sights:
			Standard / Stress Multiplier
Rep 1 Time:	Rep 2 Time:	Rep 3 Time:	
+ Penalties:	+ Penalties:	+ Penalties:	Notes:
Rep 1 Score:	Rep 2 Score:	Rep 3 Score:	
Par: Go / No Go	**Par: Go / No Go**	**Par: Go / No Go**	

Gunfighting Skills - 2

IN THE LINE OF FIRE

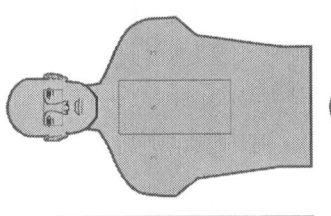
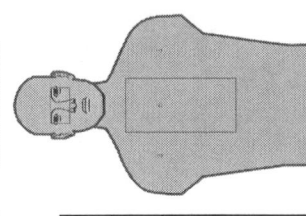

Date:	Location:	Weapon:	Sights:
Rep 1 Time:	Rep 2 Time:	Rep 3 Time:	Standard / Stress Multiplier
+ Penalties:	+ Penalties:	+ Penalties:	
Rep 1 Score:	Rep 2 Score:	Rep 3 Score:	Notes:
Par: Go / No Go	**Par: Go / No Go**	**Par: Go / No Go**	

Date:	Location:	Weapon:	Sights:
Rep 1 Time:	Rep 2 Time:	Rep 3 Time:	Standard / Stress Multiplier
+ Penalties:	+ Penalties:	+ Penalties:	
Rep 1 Score:	Rep 2 Score:	Rep 3 Score:	Notes:
Par: Go / No Go	**Par: Go / No Go**	**Par: Go / No Go**	

Date:	Location:	Weapon:	Sights:
Rep 1 Time:	Rep 2 Time:	Rep 3 Time:	Standard / Stress Multiplier
+ Penalties:	+ Penalties:	+ Penalties:	
Rep 1 Score:	Rep 2 Score:	Rep 3 Score:	Notes:
Par: Go / No Go	**Par: Go / No Go**	**Par: Go / No Go**	

IN THE LINE OF FIRE

Date:	Location:	Weapon:	Sights:
Rep 1 Time:	Rep 2 Time:	Rep 3 Time:	Standard / Stress Multiplier
+ Penalties:	+ Penalties:	+ Penalties:	
Rep 1 Score:	Rep 2 Score:	Rep 3 Score:	Notes:
Par: Go / No Go	**Par: Go / No Go**	**Par: Go / No Go**	

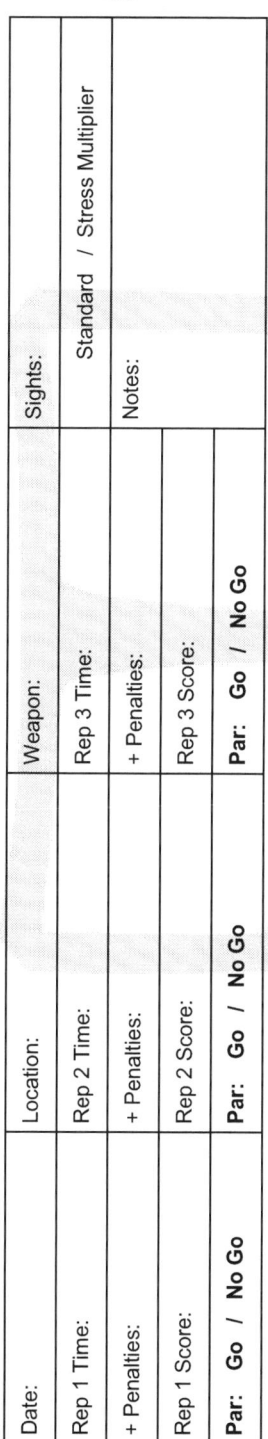

Date:	Location:	Weapon:	Sights:
Rep 1 Time:	Rep 2 Time:	Rep 3 Time:	Standard / Stress Multiplier
+ Penalties:	+ Penalties:	+ Penalties:	
Rep 1 Score:	Rep 2 Score:	Rep 3 Score:	Notes:
Par: Go / No Go	**Par: Go / No Go**	**Par: Go / No Go**	

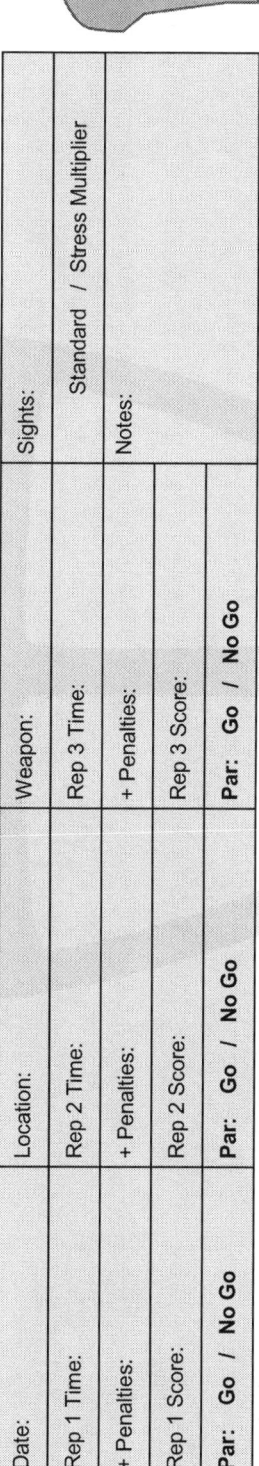

Date:	Location:	Weapon:	Sights:
Rep 1 Time:	Rep 2 Time:	Rep 3 Time:	Standard / Stress Multiplier
+ Penalties:	+ Penalties:	+ Penalties:	
Rep 1 Score:	Rep 2 Score:	Rep 3 Score:	Notes:
Par: Go / No Go	**Par: Go / No Go**	**Par: Go / No Go**	

Fundamental Carbine ©

IN THE LINE OF FIRE

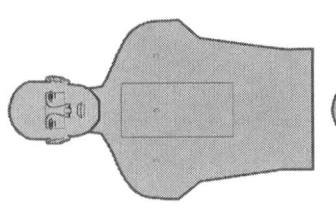
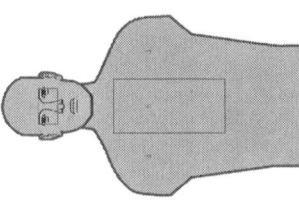

www.GUNFIGHTERSERIES.com ©

Date:	Location:	Weapon:	Sights:
Rep 1 Time:	Rep 2 Time:	Rep 3 Time:	Standard / Stress Multiplier
+ Penalties:	+ Penalties:	+ Penalties:	
Rep 1 Score:	Rep 2 Score:	Rep 3 Score:	Notes:
Par: Go / No Go	**Par: Go / No Go**	**Par: Go / No Go**	

Date:	Location:	Weapon:	Sights:
Rep 1 Time:	Rep 2 Time:	Rep 3 Time:	Standard / Stress Multiplier
+ Penalties:	+ Penalties:	+ Penalties:	
Rep 1 Score:	Rep 2 Score:	Rep 3 Score:	Notes:
Par: Go / No Go	**Par: Go / No Go**	**Par: Go / No Go**	

Date:	Location:	Weapon:	Sights:
Rep 1 Time:	Rep 2 Time:	Rep 3 Time:	Standard / Stress Multiplier
+ Penalties:	+ Penalties:	+ Penalties:	
Rep 1 Score:	Rep 2 Score:	Rep 3 Score:	Notes:
Par: Go / No Go	**Par: Go / No Go**	**Par: Go / No Go**	

IN THE LINE OF FIRE

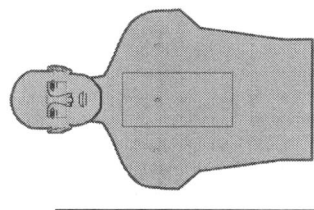

Date:	Location:	Weapon:	Sights:
Rep 1 Time:	Rep 2 Time:	Rep 3 Time:	Standard / Stress Multiplier
+ Penalties:	+ Penalties:	+ Penalties:	
Rep 1 Score:	Rep 2 Score:	Rep 3 Score:	Notes:
Par: Go / No Go	**Par: Go / No Go**	**Par: Go / No Go**	

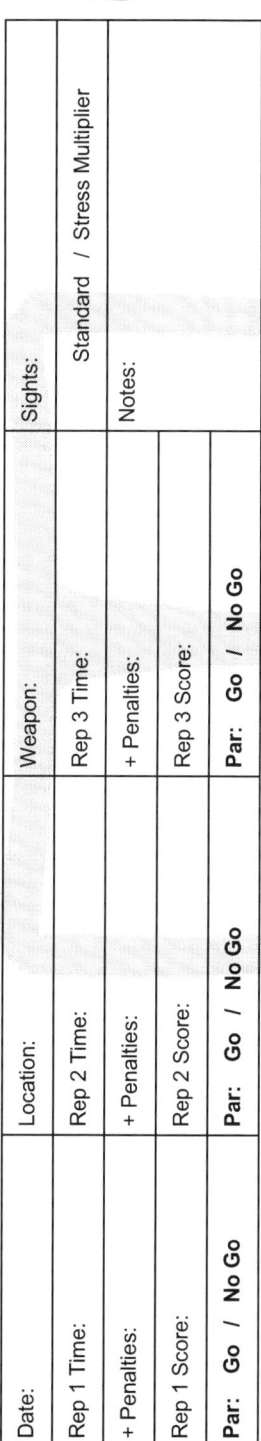

Date:	Location:	Weapon:	Sights:
Rep 1 Time:	Rep 2 Time:	Rep 3 Time:	Standard / Stress Multiplier
+ Penalties:	+ Penalties:	+ Penalties:	
Rep 1 Score:	Rep 2 Score:	Rep 3 Score:	Notes:
Par: Go / No Go	**Par: Go / No Go**	**Par: Go / No Go**	

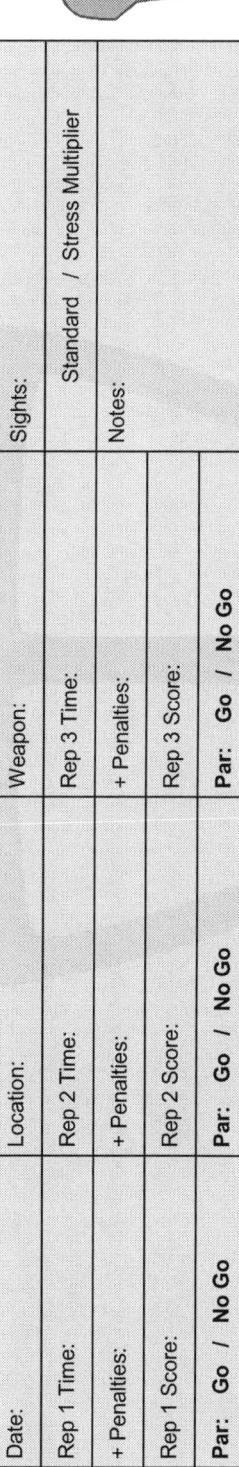

Date:	Location:	Weapon:	Sights:
Rep 1 Time:	Rep 2 Time:	Rep 3 Time:	Standard / Stress Multiplier
+ Penalties:	+ Penalties:	+ Penalties:	
Rep 1 Score:	Rep 2 Score:	Rep 3 Score:	Notes:
Par: Go / No Go	**Par: Go / No Go**	**Par: Go / No Go**	

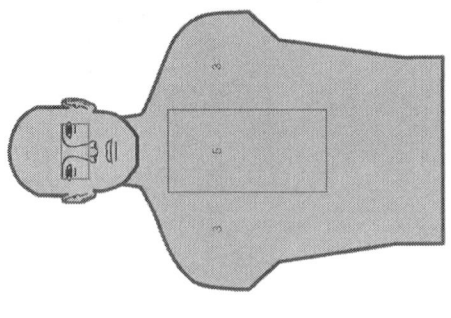

SERVICE TIME

Purpose: Increase accuracy while under pressure from emergency reload and using different positions.

Distance: 35 Yards.

Target: JD-QUAL1

Par Time: 20 Seconds.

Extra Equipment Needed: Shot timer, 2 magazines, 1 magazine pouch.

Total Rounds Fired: 15 Rounds.

Point Penalty: Go / No Go.

Starting Position & Condition: Standing – Low ready. Condition 1 with 1 round in the chamber and 9 rounds in the magazine.

Description: At the timer beep, fire 5 rounds into the A Zone (5 point) body while standing. Go to a kneeling position; fire 5 rounds into the A Zone (5 point) body box. Perform an emergency reload while in the kneeling position. Stand and fire 5 rounds into the A Zone (5 point) body box after emergency reload. For every hit in the 3 scoring zone add 2 seconds to your time. For every hit in the 0 scoring zone add 5 seconds to your time. Not making par time, with penalty points added, is a No Go of the drill.

Left handed shooter's add .5 seconds to par time and/or add .5 seconds to par time if loading from a vest mag pouch.

Variations: Stress multiplier - Immediately before the start of the drill, run 50 yards or do 2X25 yard shuttle runs, do 10 push-ups or 10 jumping jacks to get your heart rate up.

SERVICE TIME

Date:	Location:	Weapon:	Sights:
Standard / Stress Multiplier	Time:	+ Penalties:	= **Score:**
Notes:			

Date:	Location:	Weapon:	Sights:
Standard / Stress Multiplier	Time:	+ Penalties:	= **Score:**
Notes:			

Date:	Location:	Weapon:	Sights:
Standard / Stress Multiplier	Time:	+ Penalties:	= **Score:**
Notes:			

Date:	Location:	Weapon:	Sights:
Standard / Stress Multiplier	Time:	+ Penalties:	= **Score:**
Notes:			

Fundamental Carbine ©

SERVICE TIME

www.GUNFIGHTERSERIES.com ©

Date:	Location:	Weapon:	Sights:
Standard / Stress Multiplier	Time:	+ Penalties:	= **Score:**
Notes:			

Date:	Location:	Weapon:	Sights:
Standard / Stress Multiplier	Time:	+ Penalties:	= **Score:**
Notes:			

Date:	Location:	Weapon:	Sights:
Standard / Stress Multiplier	Time:	+ Penalties:	= **Score:**
Notes:			

Date:	Location:	Weapon:	Sights:
Standard / Stress Multiplier	Time:	+ Penalties:	= **Score:**
Notes:			

SERVICE TIME

Date:	Location:	Weapon:	Sights:
Standard / Stress Multiplier	Time:	+ Penalties:	= **Score:**
Notes:			

Date:	Location:	Weapon:	Sights:
Standard / Stress Multiplier	Time:	+ Penalties:	= **Score:**
Notes:			

Date:	Location:	Weapon:	Sights:
Standard / Stress Multiplier	Time:	+ Penalties:	= **Score:**
Notes:			

Date:	Location:	Weapon:	Sights:
Standard / Stress Multiplier	Time:	+ Penalties:	= **Score:**
Notes:			

Fundamental Carbine ©   Gunfighting Skills - 3

SERVICE TIME

www.GUNFIGHTERSERIES.com ©

Date:	Location:	Weapon:	Sights:
Standard / Stress Multiplier	Time:	+ Penalties:	= **Score:**
Notes:			

Date:	Location:	Weapon:	Sights:
Standard / Stress Multiplier	Time:	+ Penalties:	= **Score:**
Notes:			

Date:	Location:	Weapon:	Sights:
Standard / Stress Multiplier	Time:	+ Penalties:	= **Score:**
Notes:			

Date:	Location:	Weapon:	Sights:
Standard / Stress Multiplier	Time:	+ Penalties:	= **Score:**
Notes:			

SERVICE TIME

Date:	Location:	Weapon:	Sights:
Standard / Stress Multiplier	Time:	+ Penalties:	= **Score:**
Notes:			

Date:	Location:	Weapon:	Sights:
Standard / Stress Multiplier	Time:	+ Penalties:	= **Score:**
Notes:			

Date:	Location:	Weapon:	Sights:
Standard / Stress Multiplier	Time:	+ Penalties:	= **Score:**
Notes:			

Date:	Location:	Weapon:	Sights:
Standard / Stress Multiplier	Time:	+ Penalties:	= **Score:**
Notes:			

GUNFIGHTER CARBINE STANDARD 1

- **Ammo:** 1 Carbine magazine of 20 rounds. 1 Pistol magazine of 2 rounds.
- **Target:** JD-QUAL1
- **Scoring:** Per target score. Subtract 5 points for any shot over time. Passing score is 105 out of 120 points
- **Par Time:** 120 seconds.
- **Starting Position & Condition:** Standing. Condition 1.

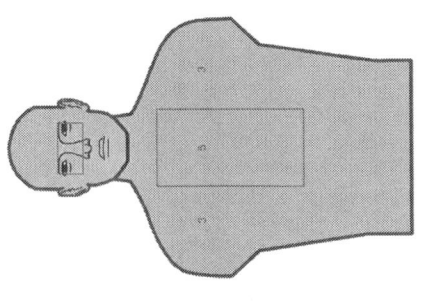

Stage	Distance	#Rnds	Position/Description
1	100 Yards	5	Standing to prone. (5 body shots)
			Run to 75 yard line.
	75 Yards	5	Standing to kneeling. (5 body shots)
			Run to 50 yard line.
	50 Yards	5	Standing to squatting behind barrier (5 body shots)
			Run to 25 yard line.
	25 Yards	3	Standing. (3 body shots)
			Run to 10 yard line
	10 Yards	2 + 2	Standing (2 Rounds head only). Transition to pistol. (2 rounds head only)

GUNFIGHTER CARBINE STANDARD 1

Date:	Time:	Location:
Weapon:	Sights:	Ammo:
Completion Time:	Under Par: Yes / No	Shots Over Par:
# of Body A Box:	# of Head A Box:	# In Body:
Notes:		Total Score:

Date:	Time:	Location:
Weapon:	Sights:	Ammo:
Completion Time:	Under Par: Yes / No	Shots Over Par:
# of Body A Box:	# of Head A Box:	# In Body:
Notes:		Total Score:

Qualification COF - 1

Fundamental Carbine ©

GUNFIGHTER CARBINE STANDARD 1

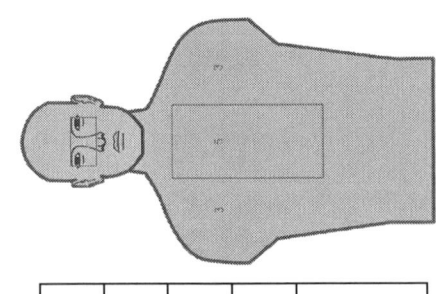

Date:	Time:	Location:
Weapon:	Sights:	Ammo:
Completion Time:	Under Par: Yes / No	Shots Over Par:
# of Body A Box:	# of Head A Box:	# In Body:
Notes:		Total Score:

Date:	Time:	Location:
Weapon:	Sights:	Ammo:
Completion Time:	Under Par: Yes / No	Shots Over Par:
# of Body A Box:	# of Head A Box:	# In Body:
Notes:		Total Score:

www.GUNFIGHTERSERIES.com ©

GUNFIGHTER CARBINE STANDARD 1

Date:	Time:	Location:
Weapon:	Sights:	Ammo:
Completion Time:	Under Par: Yes / No	Shots Over Par:
# of Body A Box:	# of Head A Box:	# In Body:
Notes:		**Total Score:**

Date:	Time:	Location:
Weapon:	Sights:	Ammo:
Completion Time:	Under Par: Yes / No	Shots Over Par:
# of Body A Box:	# of Head A Box:	# In Body:
Notes:		**Total Score:**

Qualification COF - 1

Fundamental Carbine ©

GUNFIGHTER CARBINE STANDARD 1

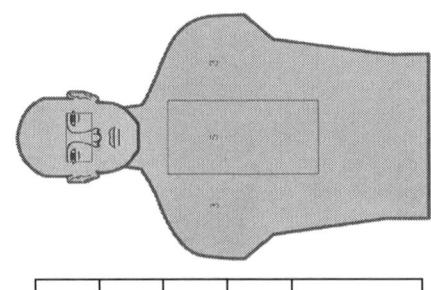

Date:	Time:	Location:
Weapon:	Sights:	Ammo:
Completion Time:	Under Par: Yes / No	Shots Over Par:
# of Body A Box:	# of Head A Box:	# In Body:
Notes:		Total Score:

Date:	Time:	Location:
Weapon:	Sights:	Ammo:
Completion Time:	Under Par: Yes / No	Shots Over Par:
# of Body A Box:	# of Head A Box:	# In Body:
Notes:		Total Score:

www.GUNFIGHTERSERIES.com ©

GUNFIGHTER CARBINE STANDARD 1

Date:	Time:	Location:
Weapon:	Sights:	Ammo:
Completion Time:	Under Par: Yes / No	Shots Over Par:
# of Body A Box:	# of Head A Box:	# In Body:
Notes:		Total Score:

Date:	Time:	Location:
Weapon:	Sights:	Ammo:
Completion Time:	Under Par: Yes / No	Shots Over Par:
# of Body A Box:	# of Head A Box:	# In Body:
Notes:		Total Score:

Qualification COF - 1

Fundamental Carbine ©

GUNFIGHTER CARBINE STANDARD 2

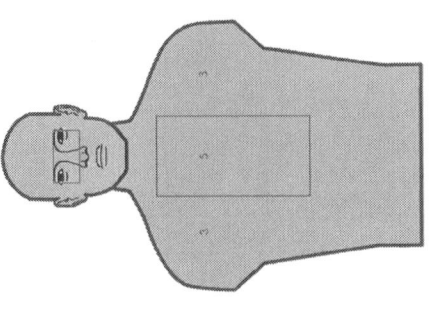

- **Ammo**: 3 Carbine Mags: 1st Mag-22 Rounds, 2nd Mag-15 Rounds, 3rd Mag-13 Rounds. 1 Pistol Mag of 1 Rounds.
- **Target**: JD-QUAL1
- **Scoring**: Per target score. Subtract 5 points for any shot over time. Passing score is 225 out of 250 points
- **Starting Position & Condition**: Standing. 1st magazine of 22 loaded. Condition 1.

Stage	Distance	#Rnds	Time	Position/Description
1	100 Yards	5	25 Sec	Standing, low ready to prone.
2	75 yards	4	15 Sec	Standing, high ready to kneeling.
3	50 Yards	4 + 4	18 Sec	4 Rounds standing, tactical ready. 4 Rounds kneeling.
4	25 yards	9 + 8	40 Sec	9 Rounds standing, low ready. Emergency reload with mag of 15. 8 Rounds kneeling.(BODY ONLY)
5	25 Yards	2	3 Sec	Standing, high ready. Tactical reload.
6	15 Yards	4	8 Sec	Standing, port ready to kneeling. (HEAD ONLY)
7	10 Yards	3	3 Sec.	Standing, low ready. 2 rounds body and 1 round head.
8	10 Yards	2	1.3 Sec	Standing, low ready.
9	10 Yards	4 + 1	8 Sec	Standing, high ready 4 rounds (BODY ONLY). Transition to pistol, 1 round (HEAD ONLY).

GUNFIGHTER CARBINE STANDARD 2

Date:	Time:	Location:
Weapon:	Sights:	Ammo:
Stage 1: 25 Sec - 5 Rounds	Make time: Y / N	Time:	Score:
Stage 2: 15 Sec - 4 Rounds	Make time: Y / N	Time:	Score:
Stage 3: 18 Sec - 4 + 4 Rounds	Make time: Y / N	Time:	Score:
Stage 4: 40 Sec - 9 + 8 Rounds	Make time: Y / N	Time:	Score:
Stage 5: 3 Sec - 2 Rounds	Make time: Y / N	Time:	Score:
Stage 6: 8 Sec - 4 Rounds	Make time: Y / N	Time:	Score:
Stage 7: 3 Sec - 3 Rounds	Make time: Y / N	Time:	Score:
Stage 8: 1.3 Sec - 2 Rounds	Make time: Y / N	Time:	Score:
Stage 9: 8 Sec - 4 + 1 Rounds	Make time: Y / N	Time:	Score:
Notes:			**Total Score:**

Fundamental Carbine ©

Qualification COF - 2

GUNFIGHTER CARBINE STANDARD 2

Date:	Time:	Location:		
Weapon:	Sights:	Ammo:		
Stage 1: 25 Sec - 5 Rounds	Make time: Y / N	Time:	Score:	
Stage 2: 15 Sec - 4 Rounds	Make time: Y / N	Time:	Score:	
Stage 3: 18 Sec - 4 + 4 Rounds	Make time: Y / N	Time:	Score:	
Stage 4: 40 Sec - 9 + 8 Rounds	Make time: Y / N	Time:	Score:	
Stage 5: 3 Sec - 2 Rounds	Make time: Y / N	Time:	Score:	
Stage 6: 8 Sec - 4 Rounds	Make time: Y / N	Time:	Score:	
Stage 7: 3 Sec - 3 Rounds	Make time: Y / N	Time:	Score:	
Stage 8: 1.3 Sec - 2 Rounds	Make time: Y / N	Time:	Score:	
Stage 9: 8 Sec - 4 + 1 Rounds	Make time: Y / N	Time:	Score:	
Notes:			**Total Score:**	

GUNFIGHTER CARBINE STANDARD 2

Date:	Time:	Location:	
Weapon:	Sights:	Ammo:	
Stage 1: 25 Sec - 5 Rounds	Make time: Y / N	Time:	Score:
Stage 2: 15 Sec - 4 Rounds	Make time: Y / N	Time:	Score:
Stage 3: 18 Sec - 4 + 4 Rounds	Make time: Y / N	Time:	Score:
Stage 4: 40 Sec - 9 + 8 Rounds	Make time: Y / N	Time:	Score:
Stage 5: 3 Sec - 2 Rounds	Make time: Y / N	Time:	Score:
Stage 6: 8 Sec - 4 Rounds	Make time: Y / N	Time:	Score:
Stage 7: 3 Sec - 3 Rounds	Make time: Y / N	Time:	Score:
Stage 8: 1.3 Sec - 2 Rounds	Make time: Y / N	Time:	Score:
Stage 9: 8 Sec - 4 + 1 Rounds	Make time: Y / N	Time:	Score:
Notes:			**Total Score:**

GUNFIGHTER CARBINE STANDARD 2

Date:	Time:	Location:	
Weapon:	Sights:	Ammo:	
Stage 1: 25 Sec - 5 Rounds	Make time: Y / N	Time:	Score:
Stage 2: 15 Sec - 4 Rounds	Make time: Y / N	Time:	Score:
Stage 3: 18 Sec - 4 + 4 Rounds	Make time: Y / N	Time:	Score:
Stage 4: 40 Sec - 9 + 8 Rounds	Make time: Y / N	Time:	Score:
Stage 5: 3 Sec - 2 Rounds	Make time: Y / N	Time:	Score:
Stage 6: 8 Sec - 4 Rounds	Make time: Y / N	Time:	Score:
Stage 7: 3 Sec - 3 Rounds	Make time: Y / N	Time:	Score:
Stage 8: 1.3 Sec - 2 Rounds	Make time: Y / N	Time:	Score:
Stage 9: 8 Sec - 4 + 1 Rounds	Make time: Y / N	Time:	Score:
Notes:			**Total Score:**

GUNFIGHTER CARBINE STANDARD 2

Date:		Time:	Location:	
Weapon:		Sights:	Ammo:	
Stage 1: 25 Sec - 5 Rounds	Make time: Y / N	Time:	Score:	
Stage 2: 15 Sec - 4 Rounds	Make time: Y / N	Time:	Score:	
Stage 3: 18 Sec - 4 + 4 Rounds	Make time: Y / N	Time:	Score:	
Stage 4: 40 Sec - 9 + 8 Rounds	Make time: Y / N	Time:	Score:	
Stage 5: 3 Sec - 2 Rounds	Make time: Y / N	Time:	Score:	
Stage 6: 8 Sec - 4 Rounds	Make time: Y / N	Time:	Score:	
Stage 7: 3 Sec - 3 Rounds	Make time: Y / N	Time:	Score:	
Stage 8: 1.3 Sec - 2 Rounds	Make time: Y / N	Time:	Score:	
Stage 9: 8 Sec - 4 + 1 Rounds	Make time: Y / N	Time:	Score:	
Notes:			**Total Score:**	

NAME OF CUSTOM DRILL:

Purpose:

By:

Distance: Yards

Target:

Par Time: Seconds

Extra Equipment Needed:

Rounds per Repetition: Rounds

Total Rounds Fired: Rounds

Point Penalty:

Repetitions:

Starting Position & Condition: Start in the

Description:

Goals: Novice: Expert: Gunfighter:

Variations:

www.GUNFIGHTERSERIES.com ©

Custom Drill Name:

Date:	Location:	Weapon:	Sights:	Ammo
				Notes:
Date:	Location:	Weapon:	Sights:	Ammo
				Notes:
Date:	Location:	Weapon:	Sights:	Ammo
				Notes:
Date:	Location:	Weapon:	Sights:	Ammo
				Notes:
Date:	Location:	Weapon:	Sights:	Ammo
				Notes:

Fundamental Carbine ©

Custom Drill Name:

Date:	Location:	Weapon:	Sights:	Ammo	
				Notes:	
Date:	Location:	Weapon:	Sights:	Ammo	
				Notes:	
Date:	Location:	Weapon:	Sights:	Ammo	
				Notes:	
Date:	Location:	Weapon:	Sights:	Ammo	
				Notes:	
Date:	Location:	Weapon:	Sights:	Ammo	
				Notes:	

Custom Drill Name:

Date:	Location:	Weapon:	Sights:	Ammo
				Notes:
Date:	Location:	Weapon:	Sights:	Ammo
				Notes:
Date:	Location:	Weapon:	Sights:	Ammo
				Notes:
Date:	Location:	Weapon:	Sights:	Ammo
				Notes:
Date:	Location:	Weapon:	Sights:	Ammo
				Notes:

NOTES:

www.GUNFIGHTERSERIES.com ©

NOTES:

Training Classes Taken

Date:	Institute:	Class Name:	Weapon:

Notes about subjects covered:

Notes about equipment used:

Instructors Name: Contact Info:

Instructors Name: Contact Info:

Students Name: Contact Info:

Students Name: Contact Info:

Students Name: Contact Info:

Students Name: Contact Info:

Students Name: Contact Info:

Training Classes Taken

Date:	Institute:	Class Name:	Weapon:

Notes about subjects covered:

Notes about equipment used:

Instructors Name: Contact Info:

Instructors Name: Contact Info:

Students Name: Contact Info:

Students Name: Contact Info:

Students Name: Contact Info:

Students Name: Contact Info:

Students Name: Contact Info:

Training Classes Taken

Date:	Institute:	Class Name:	Weapon:

Notes about subjects covered:

Notes about equipment used:

Instructors Name: Contact Info:

Instructors Name: Contact Info:

Students Name: Contact Info:

Students Name: Contact Info:

Students Name: Contact Info:

Students Name: Contact Info:

Students Name: Contact Info:

www.GUNFIGHTERSERIES.com ©

Training Classes Taken

Date:	Institute:	Class Name:	Weapon:

Notes about subjects covered:

Notes about equipment used:

Instructors Name: Contact Info:

Instructors Name: Contact Info:

Students Name: Contact Info:

Students Name: Contact Info:

Students Name: Contact Info:

Students Name: Contact Info:

Students Name: Contact Info:

Training Classes Taken

Date:	Institute:	Class Name:	Weapon:

Notes about subjects covered:

Notes about equipment used:

Instructors Name: Contact Info:

Instructors Name: Contact Info:

Students Name: Contact Info:

Students Name: Contact Info:

Students Name: Contact Info:

Students Name: Contact Info:

Students Name: Contact Info:

Made in the USA
Middletown, DE
25 January 2020